Ruth Etchells is a distinguishe
bined the study of English lit
of her life. After teaching at a grammar school in Liverpool
and then training teachers at Chester College, she moved to
university work in Durham in 1968. She founded the university course there in theology and literature while serving as
Vice-Principal of Trevelyan College. In 1978 she was appointed
Principal of St John's College. This university college also
includes a theological training hall (Cranmer Hall), and so she
became the first lay person and the first woman to be the head
of a Church of England theological college.

After her retirement from university work, she continued to
serve widely in the Church, including on the General Synod,
the Doctrine Commission and the Crown Appointments
Commission. She remains much involved in local Christian life,
particularly in Durham Cathedral. Her books include *Unafraid
to Be* (1968), *Set My People Free* (Archbishop's Lent Book,
1996) and *Just As I Am* (1994, the predecessor of this current
book of prayers). The Archbishop of Canterbury conferred on
her the Lambeth DD in 1992 for 'services to education, theological scholarship, and the work of the General Synod', and in
2003, during its 100th-birthday celebrations, the University of
Liverpool made her an Hon. Litt.D.

SAFER THAN A KNOWN WAY

PERSONAL PRAYERS WITH CHRISTMAS SUPPLEMENT

RUTH ETCHELLS

First published in Great Britain in 2006

Society for Promoting Christian Knowledge
36 Causton Street
London SW1P 4ST

British Library Cataloguing-in-Publication Data
A catalogue record for this book is available from the British Library

ISBN-13: 978–0–281–05785–6
ISBN-10: 0–281–05785–0

1 3 5 7 9 10 8 6 4 2

Typeset by Graphicraft Ltd, Hong Kong
Printed in Great Britain by Bookmarque Ltd, Croydon, Surrey

In praise of God
and in honour of
Jeremy Mudditt
without whose warm encouragement and
consistent commitment
over many years
this book of prayers would have been neither
begun nor completed

I said to the man who stood at the gate of the year,
'Give me a light that I may tread safely into the unknown'.
And he replied, 'Go out into the darkness and put your hand into
the hand of God. That shall be to you better than light and
safer than a known way'.

Minnie Louise Hoskins (quoted by King George VI
in his Christmas broadcast, 1939)

Contents

SEASONAL SUPPLEMENT FOR ADVENT, CHRISTMAS, NEW YEAR AND EPIPHANY

Introduction

Rightly understood, everything that exists is occasion for prayer: calling us to a towardness, a turning to God our Father who is Creator of sparrow and Leviathan. The lovely curve of a snail shell, the smoke spiralling up from tall factory chimneys, the hum of the street-cleaning machine spraying the kerbside, the surge of the high-speed train whooshing over the viaduct above the streets, the pavement artist chalking out his transient beauty, the inside-out umbrella posture of the cormorant blackly perching on the river's weir, the echoing of cathedral bells, the tall Babel towers of commerce, piercing the sky with their blank shining windows – yes, even to these, could we but use occasion aright, responding becomes an act of prayer.

But for this to be so, we must play our right part. For humanity's unique gift is, in George Herbert's marvellous phrase, to be 'secretary of His praise'. And that is what our daily praying is about: making holy to the Lord what is around us, as well as that part of the world consciousness we carry within us. We trace for God the life we are part of, and offer it to Him, discovering, in so doing, the texture of prayer:

> Hushed and orderly,
> a crocodile of children
> bent on learning,
> entered church –
> a boy said:
> 'Vicar, today
> we are doing texture!'
> The crocodile exploded
> as everywhere the eager

caressed surfaces.
'Sandstone,' I said to one,
'Pine,' to another,
'Marble,' to a third.
Papers were pressed,
crayons wielded.
'Evenly now,' said Miss.
Then they went,
clutching their tracings
of what they had touched,
leaving me alone
with a paper soul
pondering the texture of prayer.[1]

This book is about some tracings of what through the years I have touched in God's world, offered as a texture of prayer. As such it is 'daily' and 'personal'. It is therefore complementary to the daily office of the Church, that vital rhythm which offers on the world's behalf its praise to its Maker, and offers *for* the world intercession in its need:

> . . . Always,
> Even in winter in the cold
> Of a stone church, on his knees
> Someone is praying . . .[2]

Our own daily converse with God takes place against the constancy of that background, and inevitably starts from where we are ourselves, in relation to him and to the world. Sometimes reluctant, sometimes bursting with joy, sometimes grieving, sometimes angry, often perplexed; but always clear that the life of God is there in that dialogue – even if his whisper is so low

I have to divest myself of all my personal preoccupations to hear it. Often it is only when I have done this that I can bring my world to him for grace.

And such taking the world by the hand, and bringing it with me to God, is as important as my own personal concerns in these prayers. That is why they share with the Church's formal public prayer the discipline of sometimes praying prayers of joy when my own heart is heavy, and prayers of grief when glory seems all around in my personal pilgrimage. I find I can use such apparently untimely prayers to remember with yearning or thankfulness those for whom such a prayer would be wholly appropriate. And such prayers remind me, too, of other times and seasons in my own life when I have experienced God's hand, sometimes comforting, sometimes, for the moment, heavy; but always, if I will let him, making safe the unknown way. Always, always, true prayer turns our eyes thus from ourselves towards our Father as we know him in Jesus, and the world he loves.

Such daily encounters have their own momentum and power, and so space has been left to make a brief personal note when appropriate. I have found that over the months and years these notes become a sort of pilgrimage diary, reminding me of critical moments of God's grace in my life; tracing how the unknown way has become known, each step lit, even if only dimly, and buttressed from such dangers as could destroy me.

By request, I have included in this book a Seasonal Supplement, with material for prayer through Advent, Christmas, New Year and Epiphany. The great festivals bring together our personal and corporate prayers in a very powerful way, so these seasonal prayers grew naturally out of the month's daily personal prayers. By request, too, I have included in this volume

xi

a few of the most reproduced prayers from *Just As I Am*, predecessor to this book, now out of print.

All these have grown from the same experience: daily engaging with God in a continuing conversation, sometimes simply as I go about my affairs, silently addressing him as occasion calls; sometimes talking to him aloud or in my thinking, in quiet times of morning and evening, before the pressures of the day have begun or when I'm wearied by the day's living. And sometimes that living itself must be the prayer, consciously offered before diving in. What matters is the habit of heart, for this is the language of eternity, whose grammar and vocabulary is Love. As St Augustine invited us:

> Begin then to praise now, if thou intendest to praise for ever . . . Praise and bless the Lord thy God every single day, so that when the time of single days has passed, and there has come that one day without end, thou mayest go from praise to praise, as from strength to strength, for ever.[3]

Grateful thanks to . . .

The Reverend Dr Bob Mayo and Bishop John Pritchard for their assistance in the publishing of these prayers; Alison Barr, Senior Editor at SPCK, for her enthusiasm and practical help; Dr Judy Turner for her unveiling of such computing mysteries to me as were essential in my producing this work (herself doing the technicalities either my machine or I couldn't manage) and for being immensely kind and supportive throughout; and the many users of *Just As I Am* who asked for its successor. But above all my deepest thanks to Lady (Grace) Sheppard for the generosity and timeliness of her letters of encouragement; and to Jeremy Mudditt, publisher for God, who inspired this whole enterprise and faithfully prayed it into reality.

The cover is adapted from the stained-glass window 'High School Annunciation', presently in the Quiet Room, Durham High School for Girls. (By kind permission of the Headmistress.)

What love is
you can learn from Jesus . . .
He will teach you to put the centre of yourself outside.
He will also teach you
to be unlimited space for others.[4]

Days

First Day • MORNING

Prayers for a beginning

If all the world is God's world, then all the world is a place in which to pray.[5]

> We are pilgrims on a journey,
> fellow travellers on the road;
> we are here to help each other
> walk the mile and bear the load.[6]

Lord, here I stand at another beginning, another turn in your road for me. As I turn to you again, help me do so in company in my heart with all those who, like me, seek to follow you and serve you. As in the days ahead I lay out before you my fears and hopes, longings and aspirations and the daily matter of my life, keep me from the self-concern that blots others out. May my praise and my petitions, my offerings to you and my rejoicing in you, even my private and personal wrestling with you, be part of all humanity's worship through time and space. Keep me mindful this day that everywhere I go is made holy by your presence; and that everything I do, from emptying the dustbin or making an early cup of tea for my loved one, to taking a decision or an action that will change people's lives, is of equal value in your eyes as an offering, when I do it to your praise.

So today, Lord, for all that is to grow from this beginning, and for all with whom I share it:

> I give you my hands to do your work.
> I give you my feet to go your way,
> I give you my eyes to see as you do,
> I give you my tongue to speak your words,

2

I give you my mind that you may think in me,
I give you my spirit that you may pray in me,
Above all,
I give you my heart that you may love in me,
. . . love the Father and all mankind.

today and always.
Amen.[7]

First Day • EVENING

Be still and know . . .

But they walked and they ran,
And they marched and they rode,
And they flew and they drove,
And they bused and they commuted.

Be still and know that . . .

But they gathered and they met,
And they communed and they congregated,
And they assembled in circles,
And lined up in rows and they organized.

Be still and know that I . . .

But they convened and they spoke,
And they shouted and they shook,
And they cried and they laughed,
And they murmured and they complained.

Be still and know that I am . . .

But the marchers went forward,
The buses rolled on,
The circles went round,
The lines kept moving.
And the shouts and the cries,
And the laughter and the sighs,
And the murmurings and the complaints,
Grew louder and stronger
Whirling and swirling
Faster and faster

Until suddenly – it stopped.

And everybody fell off.

Be still and know that I am God.[8]

Tonight, Lord, help me take that seriously:
         help me be still
         help me know
         help me *know*
              that you are God.

Amen.

A giraffe, Lord.
A cloth giraffe. I saw it at the children's shop.
Fastened flat against a wall, and the children stood against it,
And were measured.
Shouts of joy – you've grown an inch;
Drooping mouth – no change (since yesterday).
It was a sort of absolute
By which things could be measured.

And I thought of how
We measure each other by cloth giraffes:
Career success? Promotion? One inch up the giraffe.
Sexual prowess – another conquest? One inch up the giraffe!
Or popularity, troops of friends; or lots of cash,
Flash cars, nice house, the ultimate in gizmos –
Or even suitable marriage and two point four children;
Steadily we move each other up the cloth giraffe.
It is a sort of absolute
By which we think things can be measured.

And I thought of our private cloth giraffes,
For ourselves, when we follow you, Lord.
Kindness not thinning under strain,
Truth told when a lie would extricate,
Gentleness when fists curl in frustration,
Silence when the hurt and insults mount,
Patience when the world exasperates,
Holiness when temptation's strong.
They make a sort of absolute
By which we fear things may be measured.

*(till we all come . . . to the measure of the stature of the fullness
of Christ . . .)*

And then we look at Heaven's wall again, Lord,
And see you do not hold a cloth giraffe.
Instead, you smile with love, and say,
'No, you have not grown an inch since yesterday;
But you have tried with your whole heart
In the things that truly will help you grow,
And most of all in asking me for bread,
In turning to me in your daily thirst.
And so, tall or short, *you will be the right height*
When you reach Heaven's door.
For my grace is sufficient for you
  And my strength is made perfect in weakness.'

Thankfully,
It is the only absolute; the only absolute
By which we shall be measured.

Lord, thank you for that grace.
Help me grow in it.
Amen.

Second Day • EVENING

A child asked me:
'What's this paper for?'
'For you to tell God
what you're sorry about,'
I replied, adding,
'You can write or draw'.
'I'll do both,' she said,
and, borrowing my pen,
quickly drew a figure
and began to write.
'How do you spell "people"?'
she asked me –
direct and matter of fact
as if writing to God
was a daily task
hindered only by spelling.

Her question answered
she placed the folded paper
in the basket
with all the others:

'Dear God,
I'm sorry.
Help me love people.'[9]

Sometimes, dear Lord, we need to go back to being a child again
just to rediscover the basics. Here's a rule of life complete!

'Dear God' . . .   O high and holy God beyond us,
                                       yet you are 'Dear' to us like the
                                       families and friends of our letter-

writing. O Lord, keep me today holding that paradox in my heart: that you are GOD, beyond all conceiving. And you are 'dear', dear as my family, dear as my dearest friends, shaping my life with the richest and deepest relationship.

'I'm sorry' . . .   About particular things, but also about habits of the heart, a way of being, a falling short. Keep me humbly penitent, Lord: not dramatic about it, or self-flagellating, but always aware that of myself I am poor stuff, sustained in a royalty of being by your unimaginable grace.

'Help me love people' . . .   with all that entails. Those close at hand, Lord, with whom I had dealings today – at home, at work, about the place – God, shape in my heart a true and gritty loving, unsentimental but charged with your grace, that looks beyond itself always to the needs of others . . . And the wider world out there, Lord: wherever my deeds or words or thoughts, my voting or my giving or my standing alongside, can make a difference – help me make it.

Dear God   I'm sorry   Help me love people.
Amen.

O my God, I love and desire to love thee with a love pure, free from all respect of proper commodity and self-interest.

I love thee, my Lord, with a perseverant love, purposing by the help of thy holy grace and assistance never to be separated from thee by sin.

And if I were to live for a million years, yet would I ever remain thy faithful servant and lover.[10]

'Perseverant love!' O my Lord Jesus, how I long to love you like that! And if I truly want it, then you will show me daily how I may come to it. So, Lord, today, begin by turning my eyes directly to you. Before I contemplate today's agendas, let me gaze at you. Help me recall those many ways in which I know and have seen you; in incidents, relationships, music, pictures, and words, so that your presence is powerful here at this quiet moment, in my heart.

I remember _____ and how you spoke to my heart.

I remember _____ and how you spoke to my imagination.

I remember _____ and how I saw you in action.

I remember _____ and how powerfully I experienced a love and joy that was *yours*. And I look back over my life, and around me at my present, and marvel at your direct action in it, my loving, lovely, all-caring Lord. I thank you, I thank you, I thank you; and I praise you, mighty Saviour.

And now I bring this day to you, and ask for your presence in it. Much of it will be prosaic, Lord, the small change of every-day living; the putting right of small bits of chaos, whether in my work or my living-room; the tedious daily jobs – changing the water in the goldfish bowl – that have to be done, with their small tyrannies. As I reluctantly do it all yet again, help me recall that you are there in them, my Christ, for you too lived a life in ordinary most of your manhood years.

And I know that unexpectedly I may be faced with some big thing: sickness; accident; unlooked-for wonderful news; unlooked-for tragic event; unlooked-for change of living . . . O my Lord, help me root all my deepest security in my life with *you*, which nothing can remove. And help me receive those things which now seem to be my primary means of security – home, means of life, health, above all my loved ones – as the ways in which you have expressed that deeper security to me. Keep me free from all protection of 'commodity and self-interest'; help me fight against my instinctive defence of my own rights and my own desires, Lord, and look instead for that larger good which may indeed require what seems like loss. And if there come days when all is dark and 'good' seems to have gone underground, then, Lord, so shape me now that I hold to my trust in you then, though you slay me.

So, my Lord, as I go out to face this day, I offer to you all whom I meet in it, and all that will be in it, that it may be baptized by the love you have given me, the only love, from which all other loves flow. Keep me in it, for your dear name's sake. Amen.

Third Day • EVENING

> Missionaries should have heaven in their hearts and tread the world under their feet.[11]

Heaven in my heart and 'the world' trodden under my feet! All that so shames (and threatens) me about my world: its rejection of God, its materialism and arrogance, its shallowness and ignorance, its aggressive self-promotion, its violence and cruelty and apathy – and *lostness*. Help me simply to tread down like long grass and weeds all that hampers my following the straight path homeward to that Heaven to which we are called. But O, my Lord, let me beat down that long grass and festooning weeds to make a path for others too. So here in my heart tonight, help me beat down:

— all *fear* of what the world can do to me and mine, its cunning, carelessness and cruelty;

— all *seduction* of this world's materialism, its glittering values and its promise of glory;

— all *over-busyness* through over-concern with the dailiness of my little world's affairs.

And may my plans tonight for the morrow and its future, and the deeds and words that will grow from them, be your path for me through the thicket, Lord, and also for others on their way to Heaven:

— those who today have helped me, or in perplexity have shared their dilemmas;

— those of my own family who are searching for a way to a better living;

— those among my friends whose care is on my heart, and for whom I pray.

Loving Father, I thank you that you have planted heaven in our hearts. Keep that loveliness alive and vital, and help me trust my Lord Jesus Christ to bring me and those for whom I pray, to that heaven-havening at last. Amen.

I have seen the sun break through
to illuminate a small field
for a while, and gone my way
and forgotten it. But that was the pearl
of great price, the one field that had
the treasure in it. I realize now
That I must give all that I have
To possess it. Life is not hurrying
on to a receding future, nor hankering after
an imagined past. It is the turning
aside like Moses to the miracle
of the lit bush, to a brightness
that seemed as transitory as your youth
once, but is the eternity that awaits you.[12]

Lord, the weather is grey, and much of the day before me prosaic and yet time- and energy-consuming. So it is hard to hold on to that bright truth I know is yours, that bright truth I have seen and known but which so quickly slips into mists and seems to be gone. And so I have gone my way and – almost – forgotten it, too often. So here and now, Lord, I pause, hold the busyness to one side, and gaze at that bright truth.

I know you love me, Lord.

I have seen it.
I know you have cared for me, and for those I love; do care; will care.
I have seen it and known it as the truth.
I know that the world is yours, and that even our sorry history cannot, cannot defeat your purposes for us.

14

I have seen it and know it and believe it.
I know you have not only lived for us but gone through death for us and so quenched its terror.

I have seen it and know it and believe it.
So help me today to recapture the sheer wonder of that in my life. Help me to live today in the radiance of that eternity which is my destiny, my loved one's destiny, the destiny of all those who trust in you. That bright field which is mine to claim, and for which it is worth giving all that I have.

So today, dear Lord,

> help me offer cheerfulness when I am tempted to downheartedness;
> help me offer patience when tempted to frustration;
> help me offer kindness when tempted to hastiness;
> help me offer humour when tempted to over-earnestness;
> help me offer gentleness when tempted to anger;
> help me offer generosity when tempted to safeguard my interests;
> help me offer forgiveness when tempted to condemn;

– all because life is lit by the sure brightness of your love.

Be with all those today, Lord, who are struggling with life: with circumstances which seem to imprison them; with crippling financial worries; with sickness of heart over someone they love; with their own body's failings; with the incessant demands of a young family; with loss of meaning for their life. O loving Christ who endured all for us, illumine today the way that is hard for so many, with a glimpse of your bright field, so that again they find hope. And teach us how to make it our own, dear Lord. Amen.

Fourth Day • EVENING

Father of all Mankind, make the roof of my house wide
enough for all opinions, oil the door of my house so it
opens easily to friend and stranger, and set such a table in
my house that my whole family may speak kindly and
freely around it.[13]

Other people, Lord, other people: your gift to us, and yet so
often not experienced as such. So often we want to hide from
them: we want to find some secure place where we are inviolate
from the intrusiveness of others. Because, O dear Lord, sometimes we feel sucked dry by other people's demands or battered
by their arguments. The noisy and aggressive young members
of the family, the dismissive cut-offs by self-appointed experts
at social gatherings or at work, the persistent grizzling of the
toddler, the imperialism of the phone – sometimes they seem
to take over the whole of my space and leave me nowhere that's
safely mine.

'Mine' – that's the key word, isn't it, Lord? Because it's not
my space at all. It's space you gave me to live in, and when I
recognized that it was actually *yours*, I asked you to come and
live in it with me and take charge of it. And warmly, lovingly,
richly, that's what you have done. But so often old habits slip
in, and I think of it as solely mine, mine to keep peaceful and
uninvaded and safe.

And then I think of you, Lord. You demanded no private
space at all, but made the whole world, with all its inhabitants,
your space. Your prayer place was the wilderness, your table was
another's at which you were but a guest; you closed no personal
front door.

So, dear Lord, help me pray this prayer from the heart tonight. Let me not fear others' opinions and arguments, however dogmatic and dismissive, but give them space to be heard, as you did. And help me rely on you to keep me right as I ponder them. Make my home and my heart welcoming to all who seek them; give me hospitality in my soul, that I may offer space to all who ask it; and help me remember always your presence among us as I do so.

O dear Lord, bless this space I call mine. Amen.

The Prayer of the lark

I am here! O my God,
I am here, I am here!
You draw me away from the earth,
and I climb to You
in a passion of shrilling, to the dot in heaven
where, for an instant, You crucify me.
When will You keep me forever?
Must You always let me fall back to the furrow's dip,
a poor bird of clay? Oh, at least
let my exultant nothingness
soar to the glory of your mercy,
in the same hope
until death.[14]

I am here, O my Lord! now at this moment I am here in your presence. And when I have to come down to earth again, how I long to stay here, high in the heavens with you . . . So today I ask for two gifts, Lord. One, that you will give me the capacity, daily, to take moments when, like the lark ascending, my heart rises to you in passionate praise – however briefly.

And second, that you will keep me faithful in my exultant nothingness even when I'm not soaring. Though most of my day will be spent in very ordinary tasks and humble places – nothing soaring about them – I do know that you treasure my small flutterings from the furrows. So keep me singing your praise, dear Lord, whether high or low

  – in the same hope
  until death
  Amen.

Fifth Day • EVENING

Lord, born in a stable,
   wanderer on the hillsides,
Thank you for the homes you have given us:
   For a door to shut against the night
                        and its fears;
   For a roof and walls to keep out the weather,
                  the wind and rain and chill;
   For all the sources of warmth in the house;
   For power sources that we take for granted;
   For clear water running from our taps;
   For the table where we gather to eat and talk,
   For food plentiful in the shop round the corner,
   For tea and coffee and fruit juices and wine,
      as we offer each other space, care and attention.
   Thank you, Lord, for such ordinary things,
   that spell for us safety, warmth and home.

Lord, born in a stable,
   wanderer on hillsides
   with no such haven as even birds and foxes know,
I remember before you now those who have
                  no door
                  no roof or walls
                  no source of heat
                  no clear running water
                  no table, and no food to put
                     on it
   no chance to delight in the small joys of minor hospitality.

Lord, born in a stable,
I remember before you now
        those crowded in stinking tenements
            huddled in insanitary refugee camps
            under rough branches in the cold and heat
               of desert
            sleeping rough in our city streets
            hiding in container lorries to seek a safe
               country
            caught in bureaucracy as they apply for
               asylum.[15]

O Lord, in my comfort remind me of the uncomfortable, in my safety remind me of those at terrible risk, in my plenty save me from complacency, and give me tonight and always prayerful and practical concern for those in need. Amen.

Sixth Day • MORNING

Thou takest the pen – and the lines dance.
Thou takest the flute – and the notes shimmer.
Thou takest the brush – and the colours sing.
So all things have meaning and beauty in that space beyond
time
Where Thou art. How, then can I hold anything back from
you?[16]

I shall make music today, Lord, even if it's only cheerful singing in the shower. Take it and make it yours, Lord – teach me your melodies.

I shall be writing today, Lord, whether it's in life's daily exchange of emails, or a love letter, or urgent business correspondence, or a plan for saving my bit of the universe. Take it and make it yours, Lord – teach me your alphabet and language.

I shall be painting today, Lord, whether it's with colour crayons for the children or a flow chart for the firm or the front door of my house or a landscape for the Royal Academy. Take it and make it yours, Lord – teach me your rainbow of colours.

I shall be planting today, Lord, whether it's in my garden or in a window box or in the minds of those I teach or in the debates in the pub or in the multitude of trivialities of help by which I try to move the world along. Take it and make it yours, Lord – teach me the divine gardening skills.

And keep me thankful, Lord, for the beauty and meaning in life, that is your gift. Amen.

Sixth Day • EVENING

Lord, help me not to dread what might happen
Nor to worry about what could happen
But to accept what does happen
Because you care for me.[17]

Lord, the weather might be so bad tonight
That we're flooded: or iced up; storm-damaged;
Or skid tomorrow on frozen roads.

Lord, the money's tight, and I don't know whether
If things get worse, we can pay the mortgage,
And we shall lose this safe familiar shelter.

Lord, we quarrel sometimes, my loved one and I.
Suppose one day we don't make it up,
And the days get colder between us, until
One day there is nothing between us at all?

Lord, this little child of mine, so tender and small,
So trusting and hopeful and playful and joyous:
What hurts will happen? What dark clouds threaten?
And – oh Lord – if I can't protect, who will shelter?
Who will stand between disaster and my little one?
Lord, when I'm not well, just sometimes
I have intimations of mortality.
What if one day my strength has trickled away
And I can't cope any more?
Lord, what if _____?
        what if _____?

Oh my child, I have been there before you.
There is little you fear I have not seen and known.
I know the abuse of weather, I know
What it is to have nowhere to lay my head.
I know necessity and its threat to humanity,
I know the suffering of the victim and the bullying of
   power;
I even endured mortality
Because I care for you . . .
So should the feared thing happen
You will find I am there. No moment
Not even the darkest moment, stays unblessed.
Because I care for you.
So do not spend your strength fighting unnecessary
   shadows
– that is not what I gave you energy for –
But live today with your heart fixed on this one great truth
That *I care for you.*

Dear Lord, take today's little fears,
and the much larger anxieties that haunt me so.
See, I give them to you now . . .
Keep me mindful this and every day
That you, Lord, oh you, Lord . . . *care for me.*
Amen.

Moving house

When the removal man left,
table and chairs were still
out in the yard.
We had so many belongings
far more than we needed.

Holy Spirit
for whom there is room
in every home,
help to clear a way
through the clutter of possessions,
to make room for those who live there
to be fully themselves
and for outsiders to be welcomed.

Spirit of hospitality, bless all
who share meals at our table –
even if it's still
out in the yard.[18]

Yes, Lord, I know my life is cluttered; I know it seems to take a major upheaval or crisis – like moving house or serious illness or getting married or a new baby – for me to face it and do something about it.

So, Lord God, today help me to take a good hard look at all the things which declare their superfluity by being still out in the yard when the upheaval happens.

Do I have too many commitments and activities – even if they're godly ones – and so not enough time for the family or my friends, or you, Lord? Help me to answer honestly.

Do I have too many financial commitments and so am too over-stretched to be properly generous in giving, not just in times of national or international emergency but regularly and steadily? Help me to answer honestly, Lord.

Do I live too social a life, filling my time with a whirl of social engagements which prevent real relationships? Help me to answer honestly, Lord.

Do I accumulate too many things, objects I like but don't need? And how willing am I to let them go? Help me to answer honestly, Lord.

Do I take on too many official roles of responsibility because something in me needs to be needed, or I like the status? Help me to answer honestly, Lord.

In all these do I stand out distinctively against my nation's culture of acquisition and success? Help me to answer honestly, Lord.

And what does my family unconsciously learn from my way of life and its true priorities? Whatever I may say to them, what do they *see*? Help me, dear Lord help me, to answer honestly.

Why does all this matter, my Lord God? Yes, I know. Because there must be room, room, room in my life not just for my family and friends but for those who need the hospitality of my heart and home; and above all, room for you, Lord. And my cluttered soul makes it difficult for you to climb past everything blocking the door, so that you can sit peacefully within.

So let me begin this very day, Lord, to sort out the unnecessary, the carelessly or facilely taken-on – and get rid of it. So that there's room at my table for you to come and make it your table, Lord: your table with the infinite space of true hospitality. A table that *isn't* left out in the yard. Amen.

Seventh Day • EVENING

> Thank you, Lord! Father, most prayers are wanting
> prayers, granting prayers and getting prayers. But most
> people, when they've received what they have, they never
> remember to say 'Thank you'. Well, this prayer is for that
> reason. Thank you, Lord, for my friends and family. But
> mostly, thanks for loving me! Thank you, Father! Amen.[19]

So today, Lord, I too want to thank you.

I thank you that you brought me into this world safely, and protected my infancy.

I thank you for my childhood, for all love and care received then, for bringing me through childish tempests and opening for me childish delights and joys, while training my heart to grow into deeper joy and sustain harsher grief.

I thank you for keeping me safe through those adolescent years of wild dreams and longings, of vision and frustration, of heedlessness and irresponsibility, yet with their glimpses of a good and beauty incomprehensible and unattainable.

I thank you for the friendships begun then, and especially for those maintained over the years. I thank you for all the friendships I have known since then, and for those I enjoy today – for their steady nourishment, for their shared laughter and delight, and for their support in the great crises of life.

I thank you for all my family relationships, the difficult ones as well as those that delight: for all family love in its many forms.

I thank you for all the opportunities for learning more of you and of the world, which have come to me through other people, through study, through the arts, through the media, through travel, through inquiry and discussion, and through your beautiful, beautiful world.

I thank you for all that I have gained through visiting far-off places and strange cities and talking with people from other cultures. And all I have gained from the familiarity of my own home patch, the streets and vennels and country contours of my own places.

I thank you for the privilege of employment and the challenges of unemployment, for your sustaining me in times of wearisome tasking, for your comfort in times of emptiness and lack of role; for the stimulus of colleagues and the sense of fruitful tiredness at the end of a long day's effort for the world's good; for your comfort when the day has felt unused and fruitless.

I thank you for the Christian communities to which I have belonged, and for that larger gathering which is the whole people of God. I thank you for the nourishing of our life together, for mutual kindness in your name, and for the depth and height of faith and understanding towards which you lead us, not least through each other and through the worship we share together.

And I thank you, Lord God, that you made us

> hold us
> lead us
> teach us
> inspire us
> love us

and gave us the Lord Jesus Christ that we might know, love, and live life in and for you.

Today, Lord, I want to thank you.

Today take me a little further into living a life of thankfulness. Amen.

Eighth Day • MORNING

> I believe in the sun
> though it is late
> in rising
>
> I believe in love
> though it is absent
>
> I believe in God
> though he is
> silent[20]

Lord, there's many days when you might as well not exist, for all the immediate experience I – we – have of you. And yet, when in a grumble I'm ready to say that, and sometimes with passion – when cruelty is dominant and terrible things go on in the world unchecked, or natural disasters spoil hope and joy and life itself – then, Lord, I stand by your cross and I'm silent.

There's something about suffering, Lord, that makes us look in your face. And what I see there is that *you know*. You've been there. More: you *are* there. So when you seem silent and absent – the worst thing of all – I ponder your crying out, 'My God, my God, why have you forsaken me?'

There isn't a drop of suffering, including the mysterious absence of God, that you, my Lord Jesus, have not tasted. So let me, today, hold fast to that. I shall today meet all the signs of your presence as I go about my world; but I shall meet all the signs of your 'absence', too. Increase my faith, Lord, when that is how things are: increase it for others, Lord, as well as myself. And let me never, never, never, by indulging my own pain in your seeming absence, assail or threaten in any way the grasp others have on your presence here in all things. Teach me not to live only in the moment but to recognize that it crosses eternity, and you are always there in the eternal domain that is the kingdom of your grace. Help me to hold on to that when everything is dark, and there seems no reason to believe in hope and life and future joy. Help me to hold on to that not only in my own distresses, but – so much worse – in the midst of others' pain, particularly the pain of those I love. Lord, I believe. I know and claim your help in my unbelief. Amen.

Eighth Day • EVENING

And now the LORD says,
   who formed me in the womb to be his servant,
to bring Jacob back to him . . .
he says,
'It is too light a thing that you should be my servant
   to raise up the tribes of Jacob
   and to restore the survivors of Israel;
I will give you as a light *to the nations*,
   that my salvation may reach to the end of the earth.'
                    (*Isaiah 49.5, 6*)

O my Father God, I thank you that you are the God for *everyone*. All the nations. All the shifting, changing, wandering nations.

Lord, the nation invited to take your message of goodness and love often failed you: but it was among that people that you raised your only Son to be, to them and among them, that same blessing of grace for the world, gathering in all who would come to you.

And I think with wonder of how my Lord Jesus Christ must have read these very words of the prophet Isaiah and found them shaping within himself, as he grew in wisdom and stature and in favour with God and man, a deepening understanding of the vocation laid upon him.

And now, Lord, it is our turn. We in our turn have inherited that same gentle but insistent invitation to take your blessing into the world; and we too have so often failed you. Yet still your loving Son urges us by his holy and gracious presence, still your kind Holy Spirit draws us out into the world, to tell all people how it is.

And I, your child, Lord, whom you called to take in my own small life your blessing into the world, I too have so often failed you in the past, and still often do so in the present.

Dear Father God, forgive me; and engage my heart afresh with your longing that all who look to you for grace should find the blessing of your love for themselves and for the world. Teach me afresh how to speak your word and live your love, *for others*, today and through all the time you have allotted me. And bring me home at last to your heaven, Lord, not empty-handed, but hand in hand with those with whom I have shared the blessing of your love; and full of joy *for them*. For Jesus' sake. Amen.

Ninth Day • MORNING

How like an angel came I down!
  How bright are all things here!
When first among his works I did appear,
  Oh, how their glory did me crown!
The world resembled his Eternity,
  In which my soul did walk;
And everything that I did see
  Did with me talk.[21]

O wonderful, radiant, glorious God, today I bring you my wondering thanks for every glimpse you give me, through the ordinary things of life, of heaven's radiant glory. For every hint of the holiness that shines through this place and this hour if my unperceptive eyes could only see. And to see, I have only to look . . . And then like Elisha's servant I shall be astonished at the mighty and beautiful forces of holiness surrounding me, your 'horses and chariots of fire'.

Lord, I do know that Eternity is the true tale of this world in which I live, and not the transience which so grips our hearts with its sad tale of loss.

Lord, I do know that heaven's brightness is the true colour of the world you created and in which I live; not the drab greyness of so much of daily life for so many people.

And, Lord, I do know that I am *myself* part of all that radiance and glory. That you made me and those I love a part of your shining.

But I need to recover the marvellous freshness and vitality of all that in my heart, dear Lord. That child-like wonder not just at the glory of Creation – beautiful, beautiful though it is – but of the greater brightness of which it speaks, the unimaginable radiance of that unseen world to which my Earth and its universe, my little daily world and the great worlds of space and time, belong, and of which they are but the visible part.

So today, my Lord, help me look through

- all that comes to me of circumstance or human encounter, to the signs of God at work.
- each moment of pleasure, to the wonder of God who will give delight even beyond this.
- every moment of sadness to the gentleness of God who has promised he will wipe away every tear.
- every moment of hard and unrewarding toil, to the God who shares his working – and his resting – with me.
- every moment of simple beauty, through all gentle loveliness of form or spirit, to the beauty and radiance of the God of Love himself.

And keep me so seeing, Father
And help me to help others so to see
                if only a little
                if only for a moment.
And so keep us in tune with Eternity
                which is our proper home.
Amen.

Ninth Day • EVENING

> Think through me, thoughts of God;
> My Father, quiet me,
> Till in Thy holy presence, hushed
> I think Thy thoughts with Thee.[22]

Now as the day ends, Father, let me put off all its swirling hopes and disappointments, its little victories and its small but bitter defeats, strip them away, as I strip off today's tired clothes:

– *my Father, quiet me.*

And in this quiet, Father, tune me in to your presence, so that the crackling and atmospherics of my own beating mind and spirit die away, and in the clearness your thoughts crystallize in my soul.

Let me open my hands, and drop all the urgencies I was going to press on you: all the injuries I was wanting you to attend to, all the proud moments – poor, poor proud moments – I was going to display to you, even the needs of others I was going to urge on you. Help me to open the hands of my heart and drop them, Lord, all of them:

– *my Father, quiet me.*

And in this quiet, Father, as your thoughts take shape in my soul, may they become so deeply a part of me that I start to think them with you; quietly, deeply, in harmony with you, help me to think the thoughts of God:

– *my Father. Your name is Love.*

Jesus my Lord, you are depth,
Indeed my Lord, you are depth:
Having no sin,
Yielding to no evil.
Your hands sweet and clean,
Yet you became the friend of sinners,
Your love freely shared among them.
Jesus my Lord, you are depth,
Indeed my Lord, you are depth:
Loosing the chains of those who were bound
In body or in spirit,
Yet you yourself, in chains,
Went the dolorous way
From Gethsemane to Calvary. Amen.[23]

'Your hands sweet and clean.' Oh my Lord, that is the wonder and mystery of your presence here with us. I listen to my radio and read the press and reflect on my own life and am conscious that our world is sick and sinful, and I am part of it. And yet, my beloved Lord, here you are, *in it* and part of it and along-side us; not separated from us by some defensive spiritual glass wall, but sharing our nature and our life and sharing therefore all those pressures, within and without, that make us the wounded and sinning creatures we are. And your hands remain 'sweet and clean'.

And because they do that, Lord, even when you are walking our most dolorous ways, you can loose us from the evil things that bind us: from the resentment that keeps us returning to old wounds and hatreds, from the pride that needs the other to say 'sorry' first; from the greed that so insidiously is shaping our priorities, letting 'I want' replace 'I need'; from the possessiveness that corrupts our loving; from the anxieties that undermine our joy in life.

Lord Jesus, take my grubby hands in your sweet and clean ones, and set me free. Free to serve you and love you – and therefore my world – in this place and this time, as I long to do and was created to do.

And in so doing, Lord, give me a profounder sense of your *depth*, of the extraordinary profundity of grace on which through you I can draw, in which, through you, I am rooted. Help me to glimpse today, Lord, your depth:

— in every encounter
— in every circumstance, small or great
— in every inward journey I make in my mind and heart, and every outward journey I make towards my world.

Be my depth for me, Lord. Amen.

Tenth Day • EVENING

Lord, I have been struggling all day with the intransigence of things. Nothing has gone smoothly and the day has seemed full of minor domestic difficulties and personal irritabilities and I felt like a cat with its fur rubbed the wrong way. Nothing tragic, Lord: just the bumps and bangs of being human in the twenty-first century, here in the West. All the electronic marvels that should make life easier and prove recalcitrant; the phone ringing at the wrong time, the delivery man not coming when promised, the car not starting, the computer being unmanageable. People not being where we'd arranged, the TV on the blink. And the omnipresent mobile phone distracting passers-by from their immediate surroundings so that they barge their way amongst the shoppers with unconscious but real rudeness. And so it goes: *minor disorders which can question the nature of the universe.*

And then this evening I was reading Patrick White's *Tree of Man* and found a profound benediction to rest my weary spirit on this night. So I thank you for it, Lord. A reminder that behind the fractured goodness of our crowded frenetic culture lies a pattern of creation where your will for our profoundest good, O God, can be discerned. The main character, after a storm in the fierce Australian landscape he farms, has an epiphany, and 'hair plastered to his head ... exhausted,' finds himself

> in love with the rightness of the world'. And next day 'he had in his face all that simplicity and goodness that he sensed to be paramount. Why, each frond of the pepper tree could not have been otherwise.' At his death, 'as he stood waiting for the flesh to be loosed on him, he prayed

for greater clarity, and it became obvious . . . It was
clear that One, and no other figure, is the answer to all
sums . . .'

Lord, I too have had moments of sudden intense understanding and joy, a tremor of bliss, a blink of Heaven, when I knew and felt 'the rightness of the world' and how it expressed the One who is 'the answer to all sums'; and I thank you for them. O my Lord, these epiphanies are so brief and so important, so fundamental to the journey of my life. Keep me travelling true to the understanding they give when my world seems to deny radiant possibilities. Keep me trusting, trusting, trusting, Lord, in the grace I have glimpsed and known as the ultimate truth about life. Trusting in that essential 'rightness' behind the chaos, and its shaping by you, the One – and no other – who is the answer to all sums. And so bless my bed tonight, whether waking or sleeping, that awake I may rest in your sure grace; and asleep may trust my vulnerabilities to your safe guarding. Amen, O my Lord, my Creator, my Protector, Amen.

Eleventh Day • MORNING

A prayer of the Venerable Bede

O Christ our Morning Star,
Splendour of Light Eternal,
Shining with the glory of the rainbow,
Come and waken us from the greyness
Of our apathy, and renew in us your gift of hope. Amen.[24]

Lord Jesus, Bede wrote that prayer to you here, in my chilly
grey north-east of England, twelve hundred years ago, and it's
as vividly true in its faith now as it was then. The Morning
Star still glimmers before dawn in our dark winter sky; and
still speaks of the brightness which is yours, Lord, breaking
through to us when our lives are dark.

> Lord, help me to look for your Morning Star today, in
> whatever may be darkness in my life. Help me fix my gaze
> on it, rather than on the darkness; and may I find by it
> not only light but direction.

The rainbow is still glorious across the rolling grey clouds of
rainstorms, planted in our earth and rising in its great bow
heavenwards.

> Lord, help me look for your rainbow today, in whatever
> is grey in my life. Help me shake off dullness of spirit,
> and catch the glory that is there amidst the prosaic, the
> ordinary routines of my day. Take today's busy-ness, Lord
> God, and light it with your rainbow spectrum of holy
> colour.

And be with those for whom your Morning Star and rainbow
are inconceivable, who are caught in the dark and the grey, with

no shimmer of light or hint at your dazzle of colour. Give them the desire to see, Lord. And give me the sensitivity to join them in their search. And so renew in us all the brilliance of your hope. Amen.

Eleventh Day • EVENING

> Thanks be to God
> that sometimes we can
> walk in Eden. Quiet
> in the morning, I catch
> the shadow and the sun
> so neither hurt . . .
> trees there are in plenty
> arching like Blake's tall angels
> over me, each a blessing, none
> bearing the troublesome apple.[25]

Lord, thank you for those times you give me, often unlooked
for, when you open the gates of Eden again briefly, and I walk
with you there. Now, as I lie down to sleep, I think of them. I
remember:

Quiet days with friends in gentle places – by small
   streams,
or among meadows knee-high in flowers, or in small
   coves.
With ripples of a calm sea creaming over shining sand;
and knowing you were Lord, and feeling thankful.

I remember:

The best and tenderest moments with those I love:
when our laughter has been joyous and kind, our
talk thoughtful and open, our actions unselfish and
sensitive, our sense very strong of togetherness in a
shared universe; our trust in each other near absolute.
Without worm of discord or mist of doubt or inner

fraction, delighting in the otherness of the other and their nearness. Thank you, Lord, for everything good given me by

> my parents
> brothers/sisters/cousins
> friends past
> friends present
> the one nearest to me now
> partner/wife/husband
> my children
> all who currently make up my family

And thank you for those times when we have walked together under the tall trees of your grace-filled world, seduced by no serpent and tempted by no seditious apple.

I remember: and I lay me down in peace.

And in thankfulness I give myself to your over-arching Love. Amen.

Always reflect: the blessings of God are piling against my door. Up, open, and let in the avalanche of gold! Some will remain in my house with me, some will pass on through me to other hands. Ah, no, the division is false: no blessings so seriously remain as those which pass on, for how can I be more blessed myself than in blessing my friends out of the heart and mind of God?[26]

Oh my glorious Lord, so often I forget blessings are to be expected! Give me today – and daily – the trusting heart that constantly opens up to the blessings piling up in a golden avalanche outside the door of my heart. Now, at this moment, I open that door and look for what you will give me today: not in febrile excitement but in quiet certainty that you love me, and will give me daily blessings beyond my conceiving. So help me to recognize them, Lord: often, like diamonds, they are cased in dull stone, so that I don't glimpse their sparkling depth. Or they are awkwardly packaged and seem too heavy or sharp-edged for me to handle, so I don't take delivery. Let me look beyond the wrapping of harsh circumstance, Lord Christ, beyond the packaging even of difficulty and pain, yes, even of loss, to the blessing you would give me at their heart.

And Lord, when the blessings are so obvious that even I can't miss them, use them to turn me outwards, from myself and my own wants and delights, to how they may best be shared with, and enrich, others. May I this day look to what I may help to heap up of blessings against another's door. Did I do so yesterday? Oh Lord, forgive me my lost opportunities of making others glad. Most of all, help me to share with others my sharp sense of your Love at the heart of all these blessings; O Lord, most of all may your blessings to me be a bridge to others for your Love. Amen. Amen.

Twelfth Day • EVENING

Be off, Satan, from this door and from these four walls.
There is no place for you, there is nothing for you to do
here. This is the place for Peter and Paul and the holy
gospel; and this is where I mean to sleep, now that my
worship is done, in the name of the Father and the Son
and the Holy Spirit.[27]

Father God, I thank you that through the centuries we have been
able to bring to you our worst fears, and claim the sureness of
your protection and the strength of spirit you give through it.
Help me now, Father, like those who have gone before me, at
the end of my day to turn out of this room all that is inimical
to your peace in my soul:

— against fear of bodily harm or night intruder:
> *I set the victory of Christ*

— against fear of the supernatural, against mysterious
and unexplained terrors:
> *I set the victory of Christ*

— against the guilt of things ill-done by me, today or in
the past, that burden my heart:
> *I set the victory of Christ*

— against fear of my own weakness in the night's
temptations:
> *I set the victory of Christ*

— against fears for those I love, of threats to their safety
and well-being:
> *I set the victory of Christ*

— against fears for my country and the wider world, the darkness of human history and its possible end:
I set the victory of Christ

So may I lie down to sleep in peace, in the name of the Father, the Son and the Holy Spirit. Amen.

The trivial round, the common task,
Would furnish all we ought to ask,
Room to deny ourselves, a road
To bring us daily nearer God.

Only, O Lord, in thy dear love
Fit us for perfect rest above;
And help us, this and every day
To live more nearly as we pray.[28]

'To live more nearly as we pray . . .' O my dear Lord, Creator of all that is, how often I long for the noble task to do for you, and the loftiness of vision that goes with it: breaking through the boundaries of what I can see and know of you. I long for the high revelation and the sacrificial zeal that goes with a great calling.

Instead, here I am, my Lord, facing another ordinary rather grey day with its routine and its tedium and its pettinesses.

How can I learn of you, high and holy God, and serve you rightly, in the midst of domesticity and dailiness? How can I find freedom from the tyranny of little things and small demands to talk with you and learn of you, Lord, as I should? The incessant demands of the younger members of the family, Lord, and the needs of my elderly and frail: the knocks on the door, the telephone, the things that go wrong in the house, the time and energy everything takes just to sustain the ordinariness of living. And then the desperate pressure sometimes at work, where detail uncared for trips up the whole system but dealing with the detail wears me down. Sometimes it feels as though there is no energy or vitality left in me to make any offering of a life worthy of you.

Help me, dear Lord, to accept the truth I want to refuse. I thought discipleship ought to be a glorious calling: and this feels so mundane. But then I look at you, my Lord Jesus, living so ordinarily for thirty years, and I know that 'ordinary' time was of a piece with your glorious public ministry.

O Lord my God, help me translate my longing to serve you greatly, to do something beautiful for you, into those acts of cheerful and loving self-denial needed hourly in the ordinariness of life; and let me understand the wonder, that such small self-denying is of a piece with the Lord Jesus picking up the heavy wooden cross. So may I be brought daily nearer you, and fitted as best may be for the life of heaven, now and for ever. Amen.

Thirteenth Day • EVENING

Where the remote Bermudas ride,
In th'ocean's bosom unespied,
From a small boat that rowed along,
The listening winds received this song:
'What should we do but sing His praise
That led us through the watery maze
Unto an isle so long unknown,
And yet far kinder than our own?

Where He the huge sea-monsters wracks,
That lift the deep upon their backs;
He lands us on a grassy stage,
Safe from the storms, and prelates' rage.
He gave us this eternal Spring
Which here enamels everything,
And sends the fowls to us in care,
On daily visits through the air . . .
He cast (of which we rather boast)
The Gospel's pearl upon our coast,
And in these rocks for us did frame
A temple, where to sound His name.
O! let our voice His praise exalt
Till it arrive at Heaven's vault,
Which, thence (perhaps) rebounding may
Echo beyond the Mexique Bay.'

Thus sang they in the English boat,
An holy and a cheerful note;
And all the way, to guide their chime,
With falling oars they kept the time.[29]

So, Lord, in my own life's remote Bermudas, may my oars rise and fall steadily in rhythm with the praises I bring to you, as I trustingly voyage forward. May I too, Lord, *'keep the time'* set for me by you, so that my small efforts are part of a greater whole. May I too, Lord, with holy and cheerful note, identify in each day – beginning now – the simple detail of your daily mercies in my life. Amen.

The ark

Be thankful
he didn't build it in the cellar
where the vision
which became a boat
could not be sneered at . . .

His hope was built
for all to see
and jeer at.
Nails, wood, ladders,
pots of pitch, brushes,
the clobber
of a boat-builder preparing to float.

In the open
God flings his promise
across the sky
shouts
'I love you'
in the spangled curve
of sun through rain
which holds the earth
with a striped handle.[30]

I hadn't thought of it that way, Lord: that by doing what he did in building his boat in public, to the jeers of his fellows, Noah was already declaring that God loves and God saves – whatever is to come. I'd thought it was about obedience, dogged obedience through gritted teeth. And indeed it *was* about that, as – I suppose – it was with Abraham and his slow climb up the mountain of sacrifice with Isaac. But much much more it was about love. About trusting that when you, Lord, ask us to do something, its purpose is in the end about loving and saving. Even when it doesn't look remotely like that at the time.

Lord, I look back over my life and that of my family, and I remember times when you required of us this or that: and it seemed to be about obedience, and only later we realized it had been about love: your love for us sparking off in us a – reluctant? – act of obedience that grows into love.

I remember . . .
I remember . . .

And so I see that doing apparently stupid things for you, God, 'silly things', 'foolish things', as the neighbours, even our friends, see it – must be done publicly. (Not the sort of things that bring us praise – those must be secret – but the things people mock.)

You, my Lord Christ, did a stupid, foolish thing for God in public, didn't you – getting yourself killed? And you did it to shout aloud that God loves us, and God saves us. And even so the message hasn't always got through.

So thank you, Father God, for going on shouting that message of love and safety in so many ways – including holding the earth under the rain with the rainbow's striped handle. Open my eyes to that same message in your lovely world even when it isn't lovely, and in the life around me when it is really threatening.

And help me join Noah in doing the love publicly – however stupid it looks – because you want me to pass on the message and help with the safety measures . . .

How *thankful* I am Noah didn't build in a cellar. Amen.

Fourteenth Day • EVENING

I will stand at my watch-post,
   and station myself on the rampart;
I will keep watch to see what he will say to me,
   and what he will answer concerning my complaint.
Then the LORD answered me and said:
Write the vision;
   make it plain on tablets
   so that a runner may read it.
For there is still a vision for the appointed time;
   it speaks of the end, and does not lie.
If it seems to tarry, wait for it;
   it will surely come, it will not delay.

(Habakkuk 2.1–3)

Lord, so often in my life I am as puzzled to understand your dealings with us as Habakkuk was. So often good and wise people are left battered, and smoothly corrupt ones prosper: often at the expense of those who are struggling to live good lives. Or the world just seems to be in such a total mess. And that worm of doubt nibbles at my soul, 'So where is your God?' . . . And we often seem left so long, my Lord, without word or sign from you.

And then I read the words of others who have gone before me, like Habakkuk here, and find help. It's not just the sense of companionship, that others who love you, God, have struggled and cried out to you. It's that they suggest ways forward for me, too. In his perplexity about God's use of evil men to overthrow his own people, Habakkuk went to his watchtower to watch for God's illuminating word.

And that is what I must do too. But – watch-tower? What watch-tower? Where is my rampart, Lord? And I remember a preacher in a tiny chapel in a remote village of Wales once saying, 'Our watch-tower is our *faith*'.

Of course. And I don't stand there, on that strong watch-tower, on the look-out for you, God, nearly enough. For of course it isn't the poor little structure of my *own* faith we're talking about, is it, but those great shining vast walls of faith which are compounded of the Father's love for his people and their love for him, through all the ages into beyond time. I glimpse them in those marvellous descriptions in Revelation, and delight in them. And then go my way and forget *that I am already within those walls*. So, Lord, take me in my spirit up again to those strong, strong ramparts and there *expect* your 'vision for the appointed time'.

> Though the fig tree does not blossom,
>   and no fruit is on the vines;
> though the produce of the olive fails
>   and the fields yield no food;
> though the flock is cut off from the fold
>   and there is no herd in the stalls,
> yet I will rejoice in the Lord,
>   I will exult in the God of my salvation.
> God, the Lord, is my strength;
>   he makes my feet like the feet of a deer,
>   and makes me tread upon the heights.
> *(Habakkuk 3.17–19)*

Amen and Amen to that, Lord. Keep me so minded throughout this night and in the days to come.

Fifteenth Day • MORNING

> He is such a fast God: always before us
> And leaving as we arrive.[31]

We are pilgrims in pursuit, Lord; and we travel so slowly, slowly, slowly. Sometimes, even so, I feel the best I can manage is hanging in there at the back of the pilgrim column. Others at the front catch a glimpse of your robe whisking round the corner ahead, and the word is passed back down the line. But so often, by the time I get there myself, you've gone.

Only – you always come back for us eventually, don't you Lord? And sometimes you come to the back of the column. There I am, sitting by the roadside taking a stone out of my shoe, and thinking how long and tough the road is, and feeling pretty miserable because I haven't really seen anything of you for weeks and I've got a blister coming – and suddenly there, quietly, you are. Among us at the back of the column, clear and warm and heartening. And I gaze and gaze at you and then I turn to say to my neighbour, 'Isn't it wonderful that He's with us back here?' . . . and when I turn back, you are gone. But it's all right, because nothing is more real and sure than the experience of your having been there.

Lord, your first disciples found you breath-stoppingly fast, and stumbled after you in a lot of confusion. But conviction, too. And I guess that's how it still is – how I am today, confused but convinced. Convinced but confused. O my dear, dear Lord, forgive my slowness, forgive the way I get distracted en route, forgive the grumbles as I plod after you. All the dailiness of things so often doesn't seem like a pilgrimage at all. Coping with the domesticities and with work demands and with the pressure of other people's 'I want . . .' doesn't feel like a high and holy journey: you seem too far out in front. But what I've learnt is that though you often seem way beyond my seeing, I'm never beyond yours. And experience has taught me that just when I least expect it, there you will be, right alongside me, saying, 'How's it going then?' And I look in your eyes and know you know the answer, and all is healed and forgiven and sorted and redeemed.

Keep me pursuing, Lord Jesus. Faithfully and steadily pursuing. And with me, all these others who long for heaven as their home, who are struggling on alongside me. And for my nation, Lord, which has let the pilgrim routes get so overgrown and silted up: Oh revive the hunger to pursue your way again. And show me how to clear the path a bit for them. For your Love's sake. Amen.

Fifteenth Day • EVENING

> Purge me, O Lord, from all my sin,
> And save thou me, by faith, from ill,
> That I may rest and dwell with thee
> Upon thy holy blessed hill.
>
> And that done, grant that with true heart
> I may without hypocrisy
> Affirm the truth, detract no man,
> But do all things with equity.[32]

How these sixteenth-century predecessors of ours could hit the spot, Lord! *Their* prayer is still *ours*. We too long for your steer to your holy hill. We too know that our fallings and stumbling can lead us far from the way. We too know how our faith can be undermined and eroded by what life does to us, by the clever arguments of those who do not know you, and by our own habits of life. And at our best and wisest we long for you to take all this and deal with it. So tonight, Father, as I seek my rest, I turn to you for that gentle medicine to my bruised – or over-exalted! – spirit; that drawing me back to the ways of childlike faith (so utterly different from the childishness of my half-rebellious posturings). That quiet divine dealing which will purge me of all that clogs and disturbs my spirit and blocks my way to being at ease with my Lord.

And so I am freed to consider tomorrow as it might be lived if I let you live it in me, Lord. My medieval mentor has the right of it! So work in me that my heart may indeed be true: to you and to those around. That I may with wise judgement know the truth and speak it discreetly, without false front or dissembling of purpose. That I may refuse detraction, that gleeful malicious small gossip which destroys others and dangerously affects the life of whole communities. And that, unafraid of the great, and at home among the humble, I may stand tomorrow in that glorious equity you have created for us and for all humanity as your loved and valued creation.

So may I turn now to sleep tonight in peace, my life and my soul in your hands both for the hours of darkness and for all I must mentally face tomorrow. In Jesus' name. Amen.

Sixteenth Day • MORNING

Lord . . .
May your bounty teach me
greatness of heart.
May your magnificence
stop me being mean.
Seeing you a prodigal
and open-handed giver
let me give unstintingly
like a King's son
like God's own.[33]

O amazing God, what a Creation and what an activity you call us to! Thank you for your gifts of energy and vision – exploring the mysterious depths of the stars and the seas, digging back into our ancient past and computerising the future, harnessing the laws of nature, identifying the deepest patterns by which we live, social, economic, psychological, moral, political; and enlarging our understanding of them and of your spiritual laws undergirding them all. Thank you, Master of the Universe, for that spiritual law by which we all ultimately live.

Inspire in me increasingly that prodigality of spirit which is the mark of your grace and the gift of our Lord Jesus Christ. Today, Father:

— in all my dealings save me from meanness:
     help me give unstintingly, like God's own;
— in all my tasks help me work committedly:
     help me give unstintingly, like God's own;
— in all my relationships give me generosity:
     help me give unstintingly, like God's own.

64

O Lord, behind the ordinariness of today let me recognize and grow up in the wonder and power of your law. And be especially today with those for whom disappointment, bereavement, weariness or sickness makes even simple survival a struggle. Give them glimpses, Father, of your glory enfolding them. For Christ who gave all. Amen.

Sixteenth Day • EVENING

And forgive us our sins, as we forgive those who sin
against us . . . Since we are herewith forgiving those who
trespass against us, this shows that the miracle of
forgiveness, the miracle of the kingdom of heaven, is
already taking place in us . . .[34]

Lord, I have been battered today. There was unkindness, and
some malice: and there is one person who seems always on the
lookout to find fault, or to stir things. And my heart seems to
swell up with the sense of injustice, and with anger at the
wilful misrepresentation of all I was trying to do – swells up
so that I felt near bursting with the effort to hold my peace.
And so tonight I can't rest, Lord, thinking of it all.

And then as I rage I turn to you, Lord. I feel your quiet gaze
upon me. And I pour it out to you, because you've been there
and know what it's like. You know what it is to intend the good
even to the point of self-sacrifice, only to find it misinterpreted
and rejected, with sarcasm or contempt. You know what it is,
to offer care and have it hurled back at you. You know what it
is to find yourself an offence to people, sometimes, it seems,
simply for existing. And you know the sense of helplessness that
overtakes the spirit when nothing you can do or say is accepted
for what it is.

And then . . . As I tell you all this, you turn my heart from
the contemplation of my own woes and my inadequacy in dealing with them. Because as I rest my battered self against your
strength and comfort, the absolute and unconditional love you
have for me, I begin to draw from your presence something of
the way you dealt with such times. It's all about forgiveness, isn't
it, Lord? Forgiveness as the most absolute power in the universe,

because it dissolves the bitterness that can canker my soul; because it turns me to think in your presence of those who have hurt me. To look at them not as trapped in the box of my own resentments but as whole people living out their lives under your just and tender gaze – even as I am.

O my dear Lord, I do not find forgiveness easy; but I do know I *want* to forgive. Even more, I want *you* to forgive them; and to forgive me too, for just like them I too need your forgiving. All the time, we need your forgiving.

And as I pray that, I know that those words were right: that the miracle of forgiveness is happening. That right here, in this room this night, the kingdom of heaven is already taking place. Now as I receive that at your hands, my Lord, help me not to slip back into a recital of my injuries, but instead commend my soul and theirs to your protection, and so lay me down in peace. Amen. Amen.

Seventeenth Day • MORNING

(A prayer for children caught in warfare across the world)

Blitz kid, Britain 1940

(Written for a British Legion Act of Remembrance, 11 November 2005. Sometimes it is the trivial loss that focuses the terror and tragedy.)

I don't like thunder, though, adult now, I tough it out.
But somewhere inside me is the nine-year-old
Who discovered that the heaviest crashes thunder made
Were bombs descending that crumped amongst the
    houses round;
With, afterwards, the sound of glass falling,
Falling, falling, for minutes after.
And the smell of heavy dust clogging the air.
And lightning didn't sizzle from the sky
But flared in brilliance from the ground around us.
So you could smell its scorching
Before the sheets of flame that silhouetted
Black figures moving in a ritual dance of aid.
So those nights of man-made lightning and thunder
Have left their legacy.

Daytime was different: we were full of bravado
Scouring the rubble for pieces of shrapnel
(Exchangeable treasure that gave one status)
And edging up stairs hanging perilously
Like birds' ladders to nests blown away
In roofless houses.

And naked rooms, wall-paper exposed to the dusty air
With crooked pictures still hanging on the walls:
They tempted the adventurous.
Come afternoon, though, our competitive boasting
About our own domestic disastrous damage ceased
As the skies gloomed over towards another night.
Careful parents sent some of us bedwards
For precious hours of sleep before the nightly torment.
And then it was full dark, and the radio on, and the
    nine o'clock news,
And the steady unflappable so-British voice of the
    news-reader
Telling us how it was. And then to the dark dank shelters,
Wrapped in motley garments that made for warmth.

And then. And then . . .
The banshee wailing of the siren above the darkened
    town
And the droning, droning, droning
Which meant the thunder was coming again,
The thunder and lightning were coming again.
And it was very dark.

And that night they killed my budgie.
(I had never seen death before)
So – as I said – I still don't like thunder,
Though being an adult, I tough it out . . .
My budgie's name was 'Punch',
And he was green and lively,
And chuckled to me affectionately when he sat on my
    finger.
But here he lay on his back, with small claws in the air,
And he did not move when I stroked him.

So we buried him. And I toughed it out.
But now, when it thunders, I think of him,
And of all the small beings who died
Because we, the human race, made thunder and
  lightning.

Lord, forgive us for taking to ourselves and mis-using
The terrible powers of thunder and lightning.
And remember in your mercy all the small lost creatures
Who gave us their love, and died there in our dark.
And in the brightness of the Heaven you have promised
– Your Transformation Scene of our dark pantomime –
Gather them too, that they too may know a world
Where thunder and lightning are no more,
And never again, never never never again,
Will any of us, ever,
Need to tough it out.

All the children of the world, Father, as the guns spit and the bombs scream; and the poor creatures we yoke to our own deadly fate suffer for us. O Father forgive us, for so much of the time we don't know what we do. We fight wars for peace, Father, and millions die in the conflicts.

Father, be with all such today. Comfort with your presence. Bring us home to peace. Amen.

Seventeenth Day • EVENING

What if the essence of who you are is enough? . . . pay attention and wait . . . then just let go and dance.[35]

I have lived much of my Christian life saying that God loves me, but behaving as if I'm convinced he is out to get me . . . God can live with the reality that we are still sinners, even if we find it hard to do so.[36]

It's difficult to get it right, isn't it, Lord? Somewhere between being smugly self-satisfied and overly self-critical, there's this point of balance where we can live acceptingly with who and what we are – because God loves us as we are. Yet here again this evening I find I'm flagellating myself over all the things I'm not: conscious that today I have done and said and thought – even though in a small way – things I ought not. And not done, said, thought, things I ought. So I bring them all to you, here and now, shamed because they are burning me, and I feel myself an offence; unlovable . . . And yet at other times, I know, when the day has been much the same, I have sailed on complacently, seduced by achievement or flattery (including self-flattery) or simply insufficient thought.

And all the time the answer to this swivelling about between self-distaste and self-satisfaction is here in this very room with me. For I get it wrong, Lord, this night as every night, only when self, self, self is the subject of my heart. You say to me, 'Do you know I love you?' And I say, 'Yes, Lord, I know you love me.' And then you say, 'How much do I love you? What are the limits?' And so I turn my eyes away from anxious self-examination or pleased self-flattery, to you, my dear Lord. Here I simply am, in your presence. I ponder on your words and actions and life here among us; and your prayers for us. I stand there in the Via Dolorosa. I am there on that hill under your Cross. I watch beside that stone-closed grave. And I feel again that explosion of wonder which was your defeat of death ... *our* death.

And then I know again that by grace all my creeping and devouring sins, and all my small successes, are rolled up and dissolved: for your grace, my Lord, is all. Richly, wonderfully all, affirming that who and what I am is dear to you. So, tonight, let me rest in the utter security of your love for me, just as I am, right here in this place. And so freed from self to bring others to you for your healing and comforting and blessing:

— I pray tonight for all those I have met with today. I remember specially _____
— I pray tonight for all those closest to me, especially any anxious, weary, overspent, sick or misled. I remember specially _____
— I pray tonight for all those tormented by self-doubt or unresolved guilt, that you will come to them, and they will hear you.
— I pray tonight for all those who have lost the habit of truthful self-appraisal in your presence, that you will come to them, and they will hear you.
— I pray tonight for all those so weighed down by their own or the world's failings that they lose sight of your sovereign purposes of love. I pray that, caught up in the wonder of your grace flowing to and through all Creation,
           they may let go, and dance ...
           and I with them.
           Amen.

Eighteenth Day • MORNING

I have decided to obey your laws until the day I die.
(Psalm 119.112, Good News Bible)

Just occasionally, my Lord God, I need to revisit that decision that I made so long ago. I remember how my Lord Jesus told the tale of the elder son who said to his father's commands, 'Father, I go': and then didn't; and the younger who said, 'Father, no way': but then did. I said 'yes' to you long ago, Father, but I realize that sometimes (often?), unaware, I slip into going my own way rather than yours.

So, my Lord God, this morning as I look to the day ahead I ask you to direct me this day and keep me alert and obedient to that direction. May I live this day in your service, through, and only through, that loving grace which flows in my world through our Lord Jesus Christ. In each encounter today give your wisdom and gentleness; if there is harshness, enable me to bear it without self-pity or defensiveness and with a strong sense of your presence. If there is delight, help me to recognize it as from you, and be thankful. Guard my lips; more deeply, take control of my inner thoughts. And keep me truthful with myself before you, that I do not deceive myself about my own motives and actions. And when I go wrong, Lord – as so often I do – keep me thankfully conscious of your overflowing and constant forgiveness which sustains always our inner universe, as it does all Creation.

And as I go out to the day, dear Lord, I commend to your keeping all those I love and especially those about whom I am anxious; here I name them: _____

Be with them as I cannot be, guard them as I cannot, and give them today glimpses of your great and purposeful love for themselves and this whole world. In the name of the Lord Jesus who showed us what that love was like. Amen.

Eighteenth Day • EVENING

God bless the field and bless the furrow,
Stream and branch and rabbit burrow,
Hill and stone and flower and tree,
From Bristol town to Wetherby –
Bless the sun and bless the sleet,
Bless the lane and bless the street,
Bless the night and bless the day,
From Somerset and all the way
To the meadows of Cathay.
Bless the minnow, bless the whale,
Bless the rainbow and the hail,
Bless the nest and bless the leaf,
Bless the righteous and the thief,
Bless the wing and bless the fin,
Bless the air I travel in,
Bless the mill and bless the mouse,
Bless the miller's bricken house,
Bless the earth and bless the sea,
God bless you and God bless me.[37]

Your whole world, Lord God, and everything in it: the things that delight and the things that repel, the snake as well as the little owl. Your whole world, which needs your constant blessing, and our constant prayers: for when we pray we also care, and when we care we work to sustain.

Your whole world, Lord: not just the 'miller's bricken house' but the rows and rows of urban estates springing up in once green fields; and all the life of families that will happen there.

Your whole world, Lord; not just the field and the furrow, but the city centres and the networks of roads and railtracks around them, maintaining the busy life of the world as surely as the green shoots in the turned earth.

Your whole world, Lord; not just the obviously deserving, 'the righteous', but the undeserving, the unprepossessing, 'the thief': the ones who bully their way through life often because nothing in their experience has offered other forms of survival; the ones who grab and accumulate because that's the way to satisfaction; the ones who don't fit into today's mould of success – the vulnerable, the difficult teenager, the unproductive elderly, the refugee.

> Your whole world, Lord. Bless us all. Teach me how to
> express your blessing.
> Teach me to know *myself* blessed.
> Amen.

Nineteenth Day • MORNING

Lord of the morning, I do not want to rise and face this day. I am weary of the endless round of tasks, of its tedium, of the lack of en-couragement or appreciation, the weariness of grinding routine, the draining impact of constant petty criticism. And I feel so confined, Lord, by the lack of space for myself and my dreams. I feel a prisoner in my own life. Somewhere there must be freedom and light and gaiety and delight and stimulus and variety and encouragement and a shared larger vision. But in my present way of life, Lord God, I feel suffocated, trapped in a small dark room where the air is all but consumed. And then I turn my eyes to you, Lord Christ:

You gave up the infinite space of eternity,
The shining serenity of heaven;
Surrendered your power, honour and rightful glory
To the crushing finitude of our human life.

O my Lord Christ, for what? For whom?
Yes, Lord, I hear you. For us. For me.

You gave up the lovely companionships of eternity
The totally trusting, totally trustworthy loves of heaven;
Were subject to pettiness, scorn, misunderstanding,
And the limited love your friends could give you
And the humiliating death your enemies planned for you.

Yes, Lord, I hear you. For us. For me.

O Lord, forgive me. For you took to yourself the tedium and frustrations of this ordinary human life of mine, and so lived it that in it we can, if we will, catch glimpses of the glory and richness of the life within it of heaven, for which we were created and for which I so long. You showed how that life of

78

heaven was present to be lived here and now, and you opened up for us the way to do it.

O Lord, help me to grasp that truth today, so that the ordinary things I do, and my every encounter, reflect however dimly the lambency of heaven. To which heaven bring me in fullness, my dear Lord Christ, one day. Amen.

Nineteenth Day • EVENING

O house of Jacob
come, let us walk
in the light of the LORD!
(*Isaiah 2.5*)

Today, Lord, my dear inviting Lord, your prophet speaks to *me*. For we are all, any of us who choose, we are *all* the 'house of Jacob': through your great gathering in of us all as you spread your arms wide on the Cross, all heirs to the inheritance of love and light promised to any and all who accept your invitation.

Lord, we have such a need to 'belong', to know that there is some group, some family, some gathering, which includes us naturally, as by right, where we are simply 'at home'. And more than anything else, more even than the dearest human grouping, I want to belong with, simply be at home with, you, my Father God.

It is *your* people I want to belong to, Lord Jesus, king of my life.

It is *your* people I want to belong to, kind Holy Spirit, my guide through life.

And you remind me again as so often in the past that to want is enough; to turn to you with longing, and ask to be gathered in, is enough. All that is required.

So, Lord, I thank you for the moment when I first knew myself thus gathered in. No wanderings or absences since can erase the truth and wonder of that turning point in my life: from which the rest of it has been lived.

Sometimes, of course, there's a sort of weary loneliness creeps in, a distancing, a kind of numbness of spirit, as though someone has dimmed the light switch. It goes, I know, with being human and in process of being shaped for heaven. What matters is how I respond to such moments. So, Lord, I bring to you this prayer this day. Draw me back in your gentleness into your light, so that I may walk in it with your people, as one who 'belongs', who is at home with you for ever. And keep me, when such attacks of apathy or weariness or over-familiarity come, in your protection, so that I see them as passing trials, not the ultimate truth of life. And so teach me to bring such shadows to you, Lord, for your steadying comfort and encouragement, till the road is less weary and the light is restored.

And, loving Father, I pray now for those who most of their lives have felt like outsiders; who long to know what it is to belong, but are so unsure of their welcome, or so unaware of your love, that they have not known where to turn to assuage their loneliness. Send them your messengers, Father.

And in your mercy, by deed, word, thought, prayer, or just by *being* – use me. In the name and power of Jesus Christ. Amen.

Twentieth Day • MORNING

From Cædmon's song

... starlight through the planks,
God in the outhouse ...

Among the cattle, the air
in the silence, the wind
in the dust, I heard you
before breakfast, and made
this song of it. God
of the nearer presence
and the long view
I saw you, and I sing of you.[38]

Let your world and your people and my heart, my God, join in Cædmon's song of praise, along with this poet and all psalmists through the ages. Let me hear you this morning before breakfast, before lunch, before that last comforting night-time drink; let me hear you and see you and sing of you.

I sing you through history, for I look back and wonder at your dealings with us through time, God of the long view.

I sing you in this small room, in the here and now, God of the nearer presence.

I sing you in the wind and the air, the rain and sleet and sun, the silence of the moors and mountains and the thunder of the storms and waterfalls, God of Creation and my own dear patch of Earth.

I sing you in the suburbs and the city centres, the shopping malls and the shabby housing estates, the historic beautiful buildings and the broken shelters of derelict humanity, God of the heavenly city and the poor cave in Bethlehem.

I sing you among cattle and crocodiles, the hornets' nest and the squirrels' drey, the small birds in their bushes and the lion among the rocks, God of all creatures and of my own beloved pets.

I have seen you and I sing of you, my Lord and my God. Amen.

The phrase 'Do not be afraid' occurs more times on the lips of Jesus than any other, and in the whole Bible is said to occur 365 times (what does that suggest?)[39]

O my Lord, I am often afraid. I jog along serenely enough for weeks, possibly months, and then circumstances or relationships confront me with the fragility of such peace; and I find myself afraid.

— I am afraid for those I love – for their hurt, for their going astray.
— I am afraid for that love itself – that it would grow cold or selfish.
— I am afraid of circumstance – the road accident, sudden serious illness, sudden bills too great to meet, unexpected demands on my resources, physical, emotional, domestic, financial.
— I am afraid most deeply of all, Lord, that my faith in you will prove too thin when the great winds blow: and that in testing times I shall find you are not there when I turn to you for wisdom and strength.
Lord, I am often afraid.

And then I think of Gethsemane and know that you knew fear too. So you have been here. So you are here with me in my fear.

And when you said 'Do not be afraid' so repeatedly, it was as one who knew that fear would have to be faced and overcome. In Gethsemane, in Gethsemane, that is what you did.

And so in Gethsemane you have shown me how to face fear honestly in faithfulness. 'Abba Father, for you all things are possible, remove this cup from me; yet not what I want, but what you want.'

Help me, my Lord, when my fears sweep over me, to pray that prayer. O Lord, pray that prayer in me and for me, whenever I feel afraid.

And help me, living Lord, to accept the answer. Amen.

Don't

Thank you for that word.
It doesn't frighten or appal me,
just the opposite.
It clears vast oceans of
opportunities away,
and leaves me free,
not to. God or someone or
you need to say it to me
more.[40]

Lord, your freedom has so many tones of voice. Some of them I don't easily take to. So I don't always recognize that when you set prohibitions round something, it is to free me from their (unseen?) threat. Because you have freed me into the joy of your Creation and the breadth and delight that existence offers when I live it with you, I sometimes think of you only as the God who has swept away all fences, for whom the only words are 'yes' and 'do'. But of course this is not so: in the finitudes of this life here and now, with my limited understanding and faulty judgement and fragile will, beset as I am in this world as it is and as we are making it, so much that would ensnare or cripple or destroy – it cannot be always 'yes' and 'do'. So, thank you for that word 'don't'. Teach me to listen for it, sensitively, humbly and constantly. And then obey it; thankfully.

So send your messengers of prohibition to me, not just through Scripture or your Church's teaching, but through the voices of your Creation, and all that is wise and true and good in what has been written or spoken or acted or filmed or revealed to us in your gift of music. And through the wisdom of those who love me.

— Father, help me hear your 'don't' about my share in our abuse of the Earth: so make me free 'not to', whatever the cost in comfort.
— Father, help me hear your 'don't' about my share in our abuse of your creatures, bird and fish and mammal: so make me free 'not to', whatever the implications for my lifestyle.
— Father, help me hear your 'don't' in any relationships I may be in danger of abusing, any possessiveness or promiscuity, jealous pride or faithlessness, however our culture may endorse it: so make me free 'not to', not only for others' sake but for my own.
— Father, help me hear your 'don't' when many around ridicule piety, mock attempts at holy living, and make light of your name and authority, Lord God, Master of the Universe: so keep me free 'not to' even when that leaves me lonely in the crowd.

And in all these help me add my own small voice to your 'don't', that others too might hear you.

But most of all, thank you that your ultimate 'don't' is, 'don't be frightened'; *'Do not be afraid'* . . . Echoing through all your dealings with us.

O Lord God, your care of me is wonderful. Don't let me stray from it. Amen.

The dancing Word

I trod on my partners, Lord,
Again – oh! – and again,
As lumpishly I tried to dance
To your pure and delicate strain.
Your words dance together, Lord,
Swirl and drift apart;
And I cannot hold their pattern
In the stumbling of my heart.

A tune there is
Serene and small
Echoing lovely
Behind it all
And my spirit moves
Responsive, bright,
To that small tune's cadence
Dancing light.

When lightly, Lord, I fail to dance
   To the movement of your joy
I hurt my fellow dancers and
   Your pattern I destroy.
I see the rhythms broken
   The muscles tense and hard
The lovely groupings of your Word
   Grown stilted, clipped and marred.
Great shadows blur the brightness, Lord,
And spoil the flow of your dancing Word.

Let my dance be for you, Lord,
And only for you.
To that small tune's rhythm
My step keep true.
That we dance your Word together
Swirl and drift apart,
Holding its pattern truly
In the movements of our heart.

Lord, thank you for all those I have met in today's 'dance'.
I think of them now: _____

Thank you for whatever we achieved together, and forgive us all for any mis-steps or misunderstandings which spoiled the flow.

Forgive *me* for selfishness or clumsiness which in any way spoiled things for others: in particular I bring to you _____

Thank you for the joy of your dance, Lord; thank you for drawing me into it and gathering me together with people who could instruct me in it. And thank you for that small tune you sound gently and continually in my soul. Keep me true to it.

And now, as I lie down to rest, may its pure melody inform my sleep, that my dreams are shaped by its pattern and protected from all that would harm. In your name, Lord of the dance. Amen.

How terrible for us
when we ignore the presence of strangers.

How terrible for us
when the sick and the old remain lonely.

How terrible for us
when the little ones are hurt or ignored.

How terrible for us
when the prisoner is deemed
beyond redemption and love.

How terrible for us
when we do not question laws
that reward the strong
and put down the weak.

How terrible for us
when we know what we should do,
and we walk the other way.

How terrible for us
for we bring God's anger upon ourselves
and we walk into outer darkness.[41]

Oh Lord, help me to recognize the truly terrible when it is there before me: 'when we know what we should do and we walk the other way'.

Lord, keep me in all the temptations to do that now, today.

Lord, enable me to do my small part to save my nation from the walk into outer darkness.

The strangers, the sick, the old, the lonely, the prisoner, the oppressed . . . Oh Lord, prevent me, charge me, shame me . . .

that having known your love, yet I walk away. Remind me; remind my nation: that it is *indeed* a terrible thing – to fall so lovelessly into the hands of the living God. Amen.

Twenty-second Day • EVENING

> Some ask the world
>   and are diminished
> in the receiving
>   of it. You give me
>
> only this small pool
>   that the more I drink
> from, the more overflows
>   Me with sourceless light.[42]

'Sourceless light' . . . Lord, I look back with wonder. Often I wanted something bigger or more dramatic or exciting or challenging than you seemed to be permitting; and yet in this small pool where you have set me I have become increasingly aware of the depth and richness of your loving investment in your whole creation. The world is full of small places where you have worked your will: Bethlehem, Nazareth, Cana, Capernaum, Assisi, Lourdes, Canterbury, Iona . . . and this street, this corner where I live. So tonight let me affirm with thankfulness the marvellous truth that your light haloes the most ordinary lives and situations; and heaven lies all around me where I live.

Tonight, Father, I thank you:

— for saying 'no' to some of my more extravagant and ill-judged petitions;
— for the ordinary exchanges of life among my family and loved ones, for the home in which you have been with us, and for our shared life;
— for the unpraised tasks done by others all round me, for the patience and kindness of those who take time and trouble for others, often when weary themselves.

Forgive me that I have myself so often failed in such generosity.

O Lord Christ, who chose to make yourself known in a small and unimportant place, make yourself known in my heart tonight, and teach me to drink contentedly and trustingly of your overflowing sourceless light, from the small pool by which you have set me. Amen.

Twenty-third Day • MORNING

> Lord, I am lonely
> And the sun is shining,
> Listless, while the wind
> Shakes the ageing leaves.
> The harvest has been gathered
> All is bagged and barned,
> Silos burst with grain.
> Dropping bland seed
> On to a barren soil?
> Why, Lord, must I still stand
> Come, sweet Jesus, cut me down
> With the sickle of your mercy,
> For I am lonely
> And a stranger in the land.[43]

Lord, I pray this prayer for all the lonely, but especially for the old who are lonely. Those in their eighties, nineties, a hundred, for whom the savour and meaning of life has gone, along with the sweet friendships and loved families all lost to time or change or death. Lord, we all face this, but as a nation we are muddled about it. We see death as the ultimate horror, and therefore we put aside our aged ones' longing for their death as your natural release, as in the whole of the natural world. So we try to give a bit of support, with home helps and sheltered housing and even residential care. But it isn't enough, Lord, and I am ashamed.

It's not enough because we won't spend the money in taxes to make such help better. (But am *I* willing to press for such higher taxes?) But deeper than this: we won't enter with understanding into their world of loneliness and longing for release. In their helplessness – in that ward last night – their eyes anxious and humble or frightened and cowering or defiant and angry – we don't meet the challenge of those eyes. Those eyes which are windows to a soul which has produced its harvest; a soul which has seen its crops flourish and be harvested to consequences in its own farmlands and perhaps far beyond. Now its task feels complete. Winter is coming on and its lands barren.

Lord, *you* recognize each soul's harvest. So teach us the loveliness of such recognition, of joy in that life's rich offering, now almost done. Just a few gleanings to be gathered into one final collecting, perhaps. Help us to glean that, Lord.

And for the greater mystery, of why you do not gather us when we are longing so to be, help us to bear our share of responsibility for that, our strategies for keeping the weary body enduring when its purpose is gone because we so fear and hate death. Help us to see it as so many of them see it, as the gateway to something wonderful, full of warmth and light and love, full of a springtime that will never fade into winter.

Lord, help me offer that to my world. Help me with my fellow-believers tell out the glorious hope rooted in your promise. And help me trust that when you do not wield your kindly sickle even after we have ceased to intervene, there are, somewhere, seeds being sown which will bear fruit we cannot guess at.

For your weary aged, Lord, and those who care for them: your grace this day. Amen.

Twenty-third Day • EVENING

This people honours me with their lips,
    but their hearts are far from me;
In vain do they worship me,
    teaching human precepts as doctrines.
      (*Isaiah 29.13, quoted in Mark 7.6, 7*)

Therefore do not let anyone condemn you in matters of food and drink or of observing festivals . . . Do not let anyone disqualify you . . . puffed up without cause by a human way of thinking, and not holding fast to the head . . . All these regulations refer to things that perish with use; they are simply human commands and teachings.

      (*Colossians 2.16–22*)

How to get it right, Lord? How to judge which observances and proscriptions are but a human way of taming our unruly self-indulgences; not in the least important save as a template for a life lived for you rather than for myself? Fifty years ago no reverent woman attended worship not wearing a hat: and now I feel odd if I wear one . . . But it is the hard ethical questions, Father, that really trouble us, such as those about human sexuality or the intense striving after a successful career: and how consequent lifestyles mell with a life lived for you – and for others. And your Church offers me such conflicting – and openly competing – counsel on all this. So how do I stay steadily and sanely in the Way, Lord, true to what you yourself show me?

'True to what you yourself show me' . . . 'Holding fast to the head' as these readings put it. Holding fast to *you* . . . So it is by you I must test all these human prescriptions and pro-scriptions. What do you show me?

96

First, never to try to 'earn' my way into heaven by fastidious observances or excessive piety or over-zealous activity, even in good works and churchly attachment. Nor must I ever burden others, even by implication, with such things. What I *can* do is test the quality of loving required in each decision I make and each principle I embrace, recognizing always that love is not a gush of warm soapy water, but a strong clear steady flow that washes away whatever would exalt my wishes at the expense of obedience to the lifestyle you have imprinted on us by being here – washes away too anything that would threaten attentive care for others and what they can discover of you, through me, and what I do and am.

So keep me holding fast to you, my Head, my Lord. And here I remember before you all those caught in the toils of unnecessary and life-quenching observance, and ask you to free them into the glorious liberties of your grace. And equally too all those who, perhaps without realizing it, have subtly subverted the liberty in your obedience into a licensing to indulgence of the demanding self, and so are caught in a different kind of enslavement. In your pity and love, dear Lord, set us all right and keep us true, till, beyond any such questions, we are finally home in your presence. In which desire keep me, my Lord, and those I love. Amen.

Twenty-fourth Day • MORNING

JOHN BRIMLEIS BODY HERE DOTH LY
WHO PRAYSED GOD WITH HAND AND VOICE
BY MUSICKES HEAVENLIE HARMONIE
DULL MINDES HE MADE IN GOD REJOICE
HIS SOUL INTO THE HEAVENES IS LYFT
TO PRAYS HIM STILL THAT GAVE THE GYFT.
*(From an eighteenth-century tomb in the
Galilee Chapel, Durham Cathedral)*

Oh my Lord God, I thank you for the music makers. I thank you
for all those who have made dull minds – my own included –
rejoice in you. All those who with pure passion of soul have
made harmonies for us, that echo the music of heaven and teach
us the spontaneous praise that is its language.

And I thank you for all those who through the centuries, and
now today, in small chapels and vast cathedrals have maintained
that steady outpouring of praise, from wheezy harmonium to
great organ, from the piping flute and scraping violin to the
Mozart ensemble, from the cracked and hoarse voices of the
ageing to the pure soaring of the choristers: Lord, I thank you
for that continuum of praise.

And I thank you for the music of the heart, Father, which
all of us can offer though we have no voice to sing. I thank you
that you send your chorus-masters of the soul, to teach us that
inner praise, and its maintaining. And I ask that you will so tune
my spirit that it sings its small notes to you bravely and faithfully, life-long.

Dear Lord, I pray for those who have no ear for this inner
music, or, having it, do not yet know how to make its music
their own to offer to you. In your loving provision, send them

such faithful guides as that ancient cathedral organist and choirmaster, who taught the music of the heart as well as that of voice and instrument. So that all your humanity may with one voice, Lord God, one day together and for ever rejoice in your praise; and in so doing join with all the voices of your creation and the universes beyond, even to the choirs of heaven itself. Amen.

When all within is dark,
and former friends misprise,
from them I turn to You,
and find love in Your eyes.

When all within is dark,
and I my soul despise,
from me I turn to You,
and find love in Your eyes.

When all Your face is dark,
and Your just angers rise,
From You I turn to You,
and find love in Your eyes.[44]

O living and compassionate Lord! how you meet my every and deepest need! I stand among family and friends, Lord, but sometimes some misprise me and turn from me. Lord, for all those whose love I have known, before ever it turned cold, I thank you and praise you and ask you to bless them. And I know I can do this because *you* go on loving us all, unconditionally. Even me, Father, when I'm most fearful of being unlovable; even me. So when I have dark fears about my own worth; when others question it; when, even more painfully, I am conscious that I have deserved rebuke; when I *know* that I have done wrong, when I know myself most unlovable – oh dearly loved Lord, how tender and merciful you are to my bruised and grieving spirit. How you show me a forgiveness that delights in me, however sorry a creature I may be, that takes me in your arms and shines on me with love.

And so when I come to that grave place where I fear your judgement, when in awe I face eternity and know myself inadequate to the holinesses of heaven – O interceding Lord, I thank you, I thank you, that I may fear the grave as little as my bed, for there too, faced there by the absoluteness of holy justice, even there I turn to you for aid and find love in your eyes.

Most righteous and most loving Lord, be with all those today who have not discovered the love in Christ's eyes and know only a God of unpitying judgement. Break through to them with the profound reassurance of a constant and holy presence that is utterly compassionate and cares for us beyond our dreaming, even to our advocacy in the eternal courts of heaven. And help me today to be a small reflection of that loving kindness to others, in my Lord's name and for his sake. Amen.

From Hannah's song

There is no Holy One like the LORD,
    no one besides you;
      there is no Rock like our God.
Talk no more so very proudly,
    let not arrogance come from your mouth,
for the LORD is a God of knowledge
    and by him actions are weighed . . .
He will guard the feet of his faithful ones . . .
    for not by might does one prevail.

                         (*1 Samuel 2.1–10*)

Lord God, Hannah sang to you in her happiness. Against all the odds you had answered her cries of distress – 'I am a woman deeply troubled' – with the gift of a son. And you so enlarged her heart with the capacity to give, beyond anything she could have imagined, that she was able to give back to you the very son she had so long craved: 'and the child was young'.

She gave up the intimacies of those lovely years of childhood; she surrendered the pride of a mother watching her only son grow; she would not herself send him to pass through the rituals of new manhood. She would not be the one to tend him when he fell, or was frightened or sick. She would not play with him, or be the one to encourage his growing understanding, to teach him new words and ideas and to sort out the confusions of his childhood mind. All this she gave up. Why? why? – out of *joy*? Out of a sense that the God who had so answered her prayer purposed good for all who sought him, and so was to be wholly trusted?

Lord God, I find this story too searching. I can't even be wholly sure that I would have assented in Hannah's action, like that good man, her husband. But I begin to see that Hannah had caught a glimpse of the kind of God you are, and that glimpse transformed her. And, though fearfully, I should like to be transformed like that. For you too, Father, gave your only Son, out of pure love for us and desire for our true happiness – surrendered for a time the lovely intimacies of heaven, and bore the pain of letting others take your most precious one.

And so today, my Lord God, I bring my poor little arrogant 'knowledge' of the great truths of life, and put them down before you; and ask you to transform that knowledge with the greatness of your own tenderness to us. O Lord, through all your care for those who in the past have loved and served you; O Lord, through all your care for those who today love and serve you; O Lord, through all the love and care you have showered on me: enlarge my love and trust, Lord, that like Hannah, though with a quailing joy, I can offer you my greatest treasure.

My greatest treasure? Here I name it _____

Lord, in whatever way you want to receive it, help me give it back to you.

Now, Lord. Amen.

> I think that nothing made is lost;
> That not a moon has ever shone,
> That not a cloud mine eye has crossed
> But to my soul is gone.
>
> That all the lost years garnered be
> In this thy casket, my dim soul;
> And thou wilt, once, thy key apply,
> And show the shining whole.[45]

Lord God, it is transience that haunts us: we mourn it in the cut flowers now drooping in that vase, in the creatures we love who share our homes – cat, dog, hamster, goldfish, affectionate nibbling bird – whose life-span is less than ours. Most of all we mourn when those we love most amongst our families and intimate friends seem at risk. And we sense our own transience, Father, as we begin to feel the cost of years and our energy seems to flag and our mirror tells its own tale.

So, Lord, we take this reassurance to our hearts: 'nothing made is lost'. All that loveliness of the world, all that delight in persons and creatures, secured? And secured not only because it has become a part of *me*, but, O amazing God, because you hold it in your eye and in your heart for all eternity, and so, because it is ever-present to *you*, it is not lost to me either.

Help me to be so strongly seized of this truth, Lord, that I can live it out with utter conviction, sure that all lost loved ones are safe with you, and sure that my Lord Jesus Christ will bring me through to those courts of joy where I may again delight in them in your shining presence.

Lord, be with those who tonight face a 'good-bye'.
Lord, be with those who today have already said 'good-bye'.

Especially, Lord, be with those who have not known the truth of your comfort. And enable all ministers of your grace to speak and do those things which may heal and comfort and sustain, grounded in these unshakeable certainties. For your love's sake. Amen.

The great intruder

It is exasperating
to be called
so persistently
when the last thing
we want to do
is get up
and go
but God
elects
to keep on haunting
like some
holy ghost.[46]

You don't give up, do you, God? Here I am, snuggled down in my comfortable bed of a life, drowsy and relaxed. A way of being that is warm and protected and requires little of me. Dreams occupy my half-awake mind so I'm not bored. And, Lord, it's cold outside. I like life this way, safe and undemanding.

But you keep on calling. In that voice I know so well, you keep calling. Time to get up and out, you say. Yes, my dear one (you say) you needed a rest, but that need has been satisfied. So sensible care of yourself is turning into self-indulgence. Time to get up. Time to get up and out.

Lord, I hear you. Forgive my soul's laziness. Help me make the effort to shake off my spirit's lethargy and face all that the day requires.

For it is my soul's morning, and I must be about our Father's business; even as you were, my Lord Christ.

O my Lord, help me do what I have been putting off so
   long. Amen.
O my Lord, help me take on that burden I have refused
   for so long. Amen.
O my Lord, help me face that relationship I have evaded
   for so long. Amen.

Kind Holy Ghost whose will is always for our good, go on haunting me. Till your haunting ceases to be simply a 'wake-up call', and becomes instead that flow of energy that helps change the world.

Time to get up and go out, my Lord. I hear you. Now. Today. Amen.

(And O Lord, when I *think* what this might mean in my life! . . .)

Twenty-sixth Day • EVENING

O God that art the only hope of the world,
The only refuge for unhappy men,
Abiding in the faithfulness of heaven,
Give me strong succour in this testing place . . .
Remember I am dust and wind and shadow,
And life as fleeting as the flower of grass.
But may the eternal mercy which hath shone
From time of old
Rescue thy servant from the jaws of the lion.
Thou who didst come from on high in the cloak of flesh
Strike down the dragon with that two-edged sword,
Whereby our mortal flesh can war with winds
And beat down strongholds, with our Captain God.[47]

Lions? Dragons? Strongholds? Not exactly the world I shall go
out to when I leave this room, Lord?

Well, actually, yes. They don't throw Christians to the lions
in any colosseum round here – not physically. But they do the
equivalent, don't they, my Lord? Snarling and tearing in the press
and the media generally, at Christians who make a stand that
confronts shibboleths of contemporary culture. Or locally, in
some of the groups in my workplace; or in that club down the
street . . . O, the lions of contempt and even hate prowl men-
acingly from time to time.

And there are dragons to be faced too, though they're
mental and spiritual ones. Those howling temptations, those
insidious fears, those bat-winged swooping doubts, those scaly
darknesses of spirit that lie in wait and pounce on us.

And across the world, my Lord, my fellow Christians face
all the physical menace of 'real' lions, or their equivalent:

imprisonment, torture and even death in some places. For others, loss of employment, of civil status, of justice, even of their homes. For their faith. O, all too real lions and dragons for them.

And across the world, too, many innocent people suffer the dragons of war and the lions of penury and starvation, that steadily devour them. When I read the papers or watch the news, Lord, the tale is all of lions rampant and bloodymouthed, and of fiery destruction by dragons: though we call them terrorists and ethnic cleansers and greedy power-grabbing states or multi-million combines.

So, our Captain Christ, we need you now as always:
I need your two-edged sword in my life.
My family needs you.
My friends need you.
My fellow-Christians need you.
My world needs you.
We need your strong succour.

I thank you, Father God, that from of old your eternal mercy has shone in the dark and come to our rescue. And here today I pray that my Lord Jesus Christ with his two-edged sword of justice and mercy may again come, as always, to our rescue and save us from the tyrannies that still so threaten us. Threaten this beloved world, my Lord. But we know, through your grace and mighty power, that heaven is faithful. Amen.

The prayer of the goat

Lord,
let me live as I will!
I need a little wild freedom,
a little giddiness of heart,
the strange taste of unknown flowers . . .

I love to bound to the heart of all
Your marvels,
leap Your chasms
and, my mouth stuffed with intoxicating grasses,
quiver with an adventurer's delight
on the summit of the world! Amen.[48]

O marvellous Lord, give me a spirit of marvelling! Let me make my own this 'prayer of the goat', that instead of dully taking things for granted, routinely staying in safe, well-travelled ways, I may venture ever further into the marvel at the heart of your love. Let me be prepared to pay the price of effort, courage, and change in myself and my circumstances that such adventuring forward in the world of your love may bring.

And, Lord, sensitize me where I am resistant to others who do this: forgive me that I want to stay over-safely within known ways. I am so fearful of our straying like lost sheep in our dangerous world, that I sometimes close my heart to the special gifts and vision that you are inspiring in others. Remind me constantly of my Lord Jesus Christ's struggle to lead hearts into a richer and more marvellous adventure with you. So take away my defensiveness, Lord, that I may truly judge between irresponsibility and new vision, between anarchic self-satisfaction and divine prompting. And let me so delight in others' gifts and understanding that they may become for me a path to ever greater marvels of your grace. Amen.

Twenty-seventh Day • EVENING

This meadow, a soul

Left to grow beautiful
the grassy heads do gentle talking,
and as a whole move to an unseen hand,
this way and that. The size of a soul
is like this, just let to be, to breathe,
to bathe in its own space. God has every
confidence in it, resisting continual visits
to check out how it's going. It's going all right.[49]

So there is my soul, my very being, like a grassy meadow to
your gaze, my Heavenly Father. And as the farmer, having
taken those steps necessary to its well-being, then simply lets
the meadow grow in the way for which it was created, so do
you. I had not thought of the infrequency of your felt visits
to me as a sign of your trust, Lord! A sign that all was going
gently and naturally as it should and that you had *confidence*
in me. I was too busy worrying about whether I was doing what
I should, thinking as I should, worshipping you as I should. And
wondering whether it was some failure of commitment on my
part that resulted in my not hearing or seeing you very often
or very powerfully. And all the time you simply want me to
breathe and bathe in the space you have given me, given me
to be uniquely mine. And there to grow naturally in the climate
of your grace.

So thank you, Lord, for this assurance that *whatever* the passing storms and periods of drouth in my life, 'it is well, it is well,
with my soul'. It's going, in your mercy, all right. And may those
who today are over-anxious about how they are doing glimpse

the peace and wonder of your confidence in them, and rest in the grace flowing like sweet air all round them.

And in your mercy revisit us as we need it, anxious souls that we are, and inspire in us then that brief glory of holy joy that leaps in the meadow like a young foal in delight:

> Occasionally a secret breath unseen
> blows joy across its face
> and in return the soul picks up its skirts
> and makes long swathes in meadow lengths of space.[50]

Amen, Lord. Amen.

Twenty-eighth Day • MORNING

O Saviour Christ,
in whose way of life lies the secret of all life,
and the hopes of all the people,
we pray for quiet courage to meet this hour.
We did not choose to be born, or to live, in such an age,
but let its problems challenge us,
> its discoveries exhilarate us,
> its injustices anger us,
> its possibilities inspire us,
– for your Kingdom's sake.[51]

O Lord God, who gave us our Lord Jesus Christ that we might be gathered into your peaceable kingdom, help me to take this prayer into myself and pray it today in the way I think and live.

Help me, my Lord Jesus, affirm today that you are the one who saves and heals and transforms.

Help me, Counselling Holy Spirit, affirm today that in Christ indeed there is hope, the ultimate and certain hope, of life and love for the world, and grace for all our needs. Grace for our needs, my Lord Jesus; so today I turn to you and take:

— courage for whatever I may meet today;
— commitment to play my part fully in this place and these times;
— energy to confront the problems I meet, and willingness to help, and be helped by, others in theirs;
— delight in the good new things my century is discovering and inventing and creating: our widening knowledge of the universe, our improving medical care, our global help for poorer nations;

— openness to new possibilities of living as they are offered, and a willingness to accept the changes they may bring;
— enduring strength to go on in the calling you have laid upon me;
— and remembrance of others amid my own absorptions.

O Lord God, Father of us all, your kingdom come, your will be done, here, today, in this little bit of Earth that is my life, as it is, as it *is* – *always* – in heaven. Amen.

Twenty-eighth Day • EVENING

From 'Mother Teresa'

He has only twelve hours to live:
– And over this dead loss to sanity
   you pour your precious ointment,
   wash the feet
   that will not walk tomorrow.

Mother Teresa (woman of the precious ointment)
   your love is dangerous, your levity
   would contradict
   our local gravity.

But if love cannot do it, then I see
   no future for this dying man or me.
   So blow the world to glory,
   crack the clock. Let love be dangerous.[52]

'Let love be dangerous' . . . O dear Lord, forgive us that mostly our loving is a poor little trickle between firmly bricked-in banks: nothing like the living surge necessary to sweep away all that would block and hinder its flow and transform our landscape. Our loving – of you – of each other – of the world – is so *seemly*, Lord, so respectable! It barely changes anything.

And you came and showed us what the power of real loving was like, and your great ones – Dietrich Bonhoeffer, Martin Luther King, Nelson Mandela, Mother Teresa – have heard you, and lived accordingly, and changed the world.

But we don't have to be *great* to learn that lesson, do we, Lord? Because you call us to love with your dangerous love wherever you place us. *Love that is dangerous because it changes things.*

O Lord, in my small bit of the universe, help me to be brave enough to love like that: recognizing when Love's moment has come, each day, and obeying it in thought and word and action instead of nervously pulling back because it's too radical, too in-your-face, too life-changing. Whether it's dangerous to my own way of life (my priorities, Lord?) or dangerous to my community's settled way of doing and thinking (our hostility to immigrants, Lord?) or dangerous to the superficiality of my relationships (am I really loving my family and friends dangerously, Lord?) – whatever, Lord.

Teach me your dangerous love.
And make me brave enough to do your dangerous love . . .
And blow the world to glory.
Amen.

Archbishop Alcuin's prayer

One goodness ruleth by its single will
All things that are, and have been and shall be,
Itself abiding, knowing naught of change.
This is true health, this is the blessed life.
Here, oh you prisoners of empty hope,
Minds kept in bonds by pleasure, haste you to return.
Here, here your rest, sure rest for all your hurt,
Eternal harbour for your quiet anchorage,
Shelter and refuge for unhappy men
That's always open.
This is the Father, and the Son, and the kind Holy Ghost,
One King omnipotent, called the Trinity,
One love, O thou that readest, that shall be
Thine to eternity.[53]

Nothing changes, my Lord God, in human needs. They just wear different clothes. Down in the town, Lord, at night, literally thousands of young people, their 'minds kept in bonds by pleasure', are reeling from pub to wine bar to pub to night-club, seeking ecstasy and oblivion, frenetically pursuing the only satisfactions they know.

O Lord Jesus, what can I do for them?

For they too, like Alcuin's folk, are unknowingly wounded, restlessly and unconsciously seeking 'rest for all their hurt'. They want life, Lord, and joy, and colour, and easy relationships, and the experience of being one with a huge crowd, clubbing in a rhythmic response to a huge and brilliant delight that transports them.

O Lord Jesus, what can I do for them?

And the *Big Issue* folk on the streets, Lord, and that chap who sings so painfully out of tune with his guitar, in the rain; and the jobless shifting from one dead-end task to the next; and the harassed single parents trailing weary infants round with them as they try to shop and work and socialize. They want shelter and security and quiet anchorage.

O Lord Jesus, what can I do for them?

Out on the estates, Lord, the streets are littered and there's thuggery at night and the old people are scared in their houses and the place is a desolation. And in so many care homes, the old people are sad and lonely. They long for companionship and to be treated with a care that offers them dignity and respect of persons.

O Lord Jesus, what can I do for them?

I can in my own person offer them what you have given me, Lord. *I can* share with the young the colour and delight and togetherness of belonging to your family. *I can* give the homeless my support and interest in them personally, sharing not just money but friendship. *I can* offer the old companionship and dignity, within the lovely relationships of heaven I have myself glimpsed, that you make available to all of us, all the time.

Do I? Help me, Lord, to do so today in every encounter.

I can offer them the refuge and security of your love, in every practical opportunity that comes to me, and in every sheltering friendship I can give.

Do I? Help me, Lord, to do so at each opportunity.

I can offer them the kindness of the Holy Spirit for their hurts, the friendship of the Lord Jesus Christ for their loneliness, and the royalty of the Father for their dignity; as I have myself received them and can demonstrate them in what I think and feel and do and say. *Help me, my Lord, to do so*. Today and always. Amen.

Twenty-ninth Day • EVENING

In her single small room
Miss Pettigrew
  – bird bones and parchment skin –
  lives in a leaf world
  made by her pavement tree.

When the wind blows
  the moving patterns dance
  across the wall
  and lift her heart like music.

In stark-branched winter
  she feels companioned in
    adversity
and birds in April
  bring her a sign
  from that Far Country
  where she will flower, beyond
    this alien world.

And when the wind is still
  leaf shadows touch her face
  with Love that never reached her
    through human kind.

Daily Miss Pettigrew
  – shrunk from life's jostling,
  frail essence in
  a birdcage skeleton –
  wonders why she should be
    so recompensed.

> And lives, content, in shelter
> of Love enough for her
> beneath her tree.[54]

All your saints, Lord: those achieved and those in the making. And above all, those who live simple and faithful lives that are quiet and profound expositions of trust in the living God. Lord, I thank you for all your saints.

I thank you for the richness all such add to our lives, out of their own human poverty and the wealth of their faithfulness.

I thank you for all they could teach me, would I but learn.

I thank you for their prayers, whose depth undergirds me in dark times, whose steadiness supports me when the great winds blow and whose wisdom directs me in the mists and fogs of life.

And especially, today, I ask you to let me learn from the simple saints I know who, like Miss Pettigrew, live contented in the shadow of your great Tree; finding in it the gentle touch of heaven when life is shadowed, companionship in adversity, and Love's dancing laughter and music. And springtime signs from that Far Country, where all of us may one day bear a blossoming hidden from us now.

Lord, I honour your simple saints. Help me be like them. Amen.

Thirtieth Day • MORNING

> Will you come and follow me
> If I but call your name?
> Will you go where you don't know
> And never be the same?
> Will you let my love be shown
> Will you let my love be known
> Will you let my life be grown
> In you and you in me?[55]

Will I, Lord? Will I? Long ago you called me and I offered my life to you. And you accepted it. And ever since then you've led me, and stumblingly – with lots of deviations – I've followed. But pilgrim vision and pilgrim life need constant renewal, Lord. So now I lay this challenging hymn before you and ask you to disturb my way of being with it.

Help me, Lord, today: to go into the unknown, for your sake

to show your love in my life because it's there

to declare you by word and deed and being

to nurture your life in me rather than my own

Help me, Lord, today: to care equally about those who cherish me and those who hurt me (O Lord, it is hard!)

Help me today, Lord: to face others' scorn or hostility peaceably when your truth requires it (O Lord, I quail!)

Help me today, Lord:	to make life better
	— for those who suffer darkness in spirit or body
	— for those imprisoned in circumstance, in disability, or in their minds' chains
	— for those who are unlovely, whom I naturally recoil from (O Lord, help me to be *toward* them)
Help me, today, Lord:	to do all these things hiddenly, avoiding all self-proclamation
	(or self-congratulation, Lord)
	to do all these things primarily because they delight your heart
	and show *your* love
	to the world you love.
Help me, today, Lord:	to accept with wonder that you love me.
	to discover with wonder that therefore I am lovable;
	(for to despise myself would be to disparage your love)
	And so to rest secure in that love
	and let it work its wonders in my heart and life.
	teaching me with joy that you love others too.
So, Lord, help me today:	to confront all my fears with your grace
	to see my world with the eyes of faith
	– and live accordingly.

125

Lord Jesus Christ, I thank you that since you gave your self for me, neither I nor the world need ever be the same. Hold me in the power of that wonder. Amen.

Thirtieth Day • EVENING

The widow's mites

Two mites, two drops (yet all her house and land)
Falls from a steady heart, though trembling hand.
The others' wanton wealth foams high, and brave,
The others cast away, she only gave.[56]

Oh Lord, I am indicted. Like the conscientious Pharisee, I pay my quotient of charitable giving; and, heart-moved, dig in my pocket for major disasters. And *of course* belong to the weekly giving envelope scheme in my church . . .

But that's not *giving*, Lord, is it? Not giving as that widow woman gave? Your eyes saw not just her circumstances but her heart. And they see mine. What I do is pay God's taxes – conscientiously, reasonably, reliably. Nothing more. But she gave through the pain-barrier; and you saw her as one who was at home in heaven.

It has to be a habit of the heart, hasn't it, Lord? A way of being that is wholly grounded in you, and your way of offering not just all that you had but all that you were; yourself. It means being prepared – if you ask it – to cling to nothing, but to offer it to you, my Lord, through whatever channel you choose. For that little elderly widow the way of giving was the Temple Treasury. She felt God had told her to give, even everything: so she did. She must, as she did so, have wondered how she would eat in the coming week. But she trusted her God for that.

And the widow who shared with Elijah not simply the last food for herself but, agonizingly harder, the last food for her son. Surely heart-sick, nevertheless she did it, because she was sure of God's command. In human fear and distress she gave

128

literally all she had to sustain life. And tremblingly she nevertheless trusted her God.

Oh my Lord God, raise within my heart such a longing to be like Jesus that step by step I learn to hold nothing back. That slowly I learn to give everything, as and when you require it. Starting with today, Lord. What is it you want me to surrender today? Show me, show me, my Lord: and whatever fears it raises in me, help me to trust, and give. And give. And give. Amen.

Thirty-first Day • MORNING

Time to go . . .

Time to go.
Go out,
go home,
go away.
Reluctant or eager,
fearful or full of hope,
it's time to go.

Spirit of the Way,
may we carry with us
— oil of kindness for the bitter partings
— salt of courage for uphill struggle
— spice of delight for new surroundings
— water of refreshment for parched imaginations
and sweet grace to surrender all we cannot finish
into other hands.

Time to go.

For you, God, are all around me on every side.
Before me and behind me, your hand is upon me.
And you know my ways and you search me out.[57]

Chapters open and close in our lives, Father, and sometimes we don't want them to. Sometimes we try to hang on to the particular phase in life that is ending because we can't bear the thought of not enjoying it any longer. Our children suddenly are no longer the engaging youngsters eagerly sharing things with us, but independent, often withdrawn uncommunicative beings whom we hardly seem to know. And we want to hold on to their childhood. Or we've had a particular job or responsibility that has really given us satisfaction, and then it's taken from us – perhaps through retirement – and we feel bitter and resentful about it. Or our homes have for a time been in pleasant places, and then we find ourselves moved to somewhere far less delightful. We don't want the party to end, Lord, and so we try to stay on and on, long after we should have said, with genuine gratitude, 'thank you', and gone our way.

Lord, help me to open my hands and let go, when the time has come, with simple gratitude for what I have enjoyed, and with no bitterness that it is mine no more.

Teach me, Lord, that because I am on pilgrimage it is *always* 'time to go' . . .

— *onwards in pilgrimage*, always looking forward with you, Lord, in my thinking and praying and growing and being.
— *onwards* in all relationships, with thankfulness for those of joyous love, with commitment in the difficult, with forgiving and longing in the hurtful.
— *onwards* in whatever work you have given me to do, gainful or unpaid, pleasurable or unrewarding, easy or wearisome, appreciated or unrecognized.
— *onwards* in learning more from you and about you and with you and in you.
— *onwards* in belief that you will one day bring me to heaven, Lord, to be utterly and freely with you and those I love who have gone ahead, in all the glories and amid all the joys you have promised.

Time to go . . .

Yes, Lord. I'm coming . . . Keep me going!

Amen.

Blessed is the soul that never forgets, nor lets go, of the child Jesus. More blessed still that soul which ever meditates on the grown Jesus. But most blessed is that soul which ever contemplates the immense Jesus. And so let the son of God grow in thee, for he is formed in thee. Let him become immense in thee and from thee. And may he become a great smile and perfect joy which no-one can take from thee.[58]

So at the end of this bit of the way, Lord God, as I look back, help me to think big; help me to think glorious . . .

Thank you that I have met and sat by the child Jesus during these last weeks. Bless all those little ones in whom I have met him. Bless all those who, like myself, had heard of the wonder of his coming, and went with joy to worship him.

Thank you that I have met, and been stirred and moved and challenged by, the grown Jesus, during these last weeks. Bless to me those tears he drew from me, bless to me the delight he showed me, bless in me the task he laid upon me. Be with all those tonight who have also met the grown Jesus and have been invited to join him on the Way. Grant to us all the courage and commitment for it we can learn only from him.

And now, Lord God, in wondering thankfulness I kneel before the immense Jesus. Break open the small container in which I try to hold him, thrust aside my tape-measure of definitions, let him hugely surpass my timid expectations of him. May he fill my sky, may his arms opened wide reach my earth's far horizons, may he be to me always *more than* . . .

And so may his immensity shape my soul that slowly, slowly I learn to leave littleness of spirit behind, and trust to the immeasurable surge of his love wherever it may sweep me.

And I pray tonight for all those who have also met the immense Jesus, who in fear and hope are clinging to the vast span of his garment. Help us all remain faithful to what we have glimpsed.

And so tonight may he become, here in my heart and out in the world among his people, a great smile and a perfect joy. Amen.

---

*Seasonal supplement
for ADVENT,
CHRISTMAS,
NEW YEAR and
EPIPHANY*

Prologue to the Christmas Season

Forgive an old man's babble. But I am your friend, and my love for you goes deep. There is nothing I can give you which you have not got; but there is much, very much, that, while I cannot give it, you can take. No heaven can come to us unless our hearts find rest in it today. Take heaven! No peace lies in the future which is not hidden in this present little instant. Take peace!

The gloom of the world is but a shadow. Behind it, yet within our reach, is joy. There is radiance and glory in the darkness, could we but see, and to see, we have only to look . . . I beseech you to look.

Everything we call a trial, a sorrow or a duty, believe me, the Angel's hand is there: the gift is there, and the wonder of an overshadowing Presence. Our joys, too: be not content with them as joys; they too conceal diviner gifts.

Life is so full of meaning and of purpose, so full of beauty – beneath its covering – that you will find earth but cloaks your heaven. Courage then, to claim it! But courage you have, and the knowledge that we are pilgrims together, wending through unknown country, home.

And so at this Christmas time I greet you, not quite as the world sends greetings, but with profound esteem, and with the prayer that for you, now and forever, the day breaks and the shadows flee away . . . (Christmas Eve 1513)[59]

For Advent Sunday

On this mountain the LORD of hosts will make for all peoples
a feast of rich food, a feast of well-matured wines,
of rich food filled with marrow, of well-matured wines
strained clear.
And . . . he will swallow up death for ever.
Then the Lord GOD will wipe away the tears from all faces,
and the disgrace of his people he will take away from all
the earth,
for the LORD has spoken . . .
It will be said on that day,
Lo, this is our God; we have waited for him, so that he
might save us.
This is the LORD for whom we have waited;
let us be glad and rejoice in his salvation,
For the hand of the LORD will rest on this mountain.

(Isaiah 25.6–10)

Judgement Day . . . and beyond

No more grief, Lord? One day? No more sobbing? Oh, the
tenderness of your promised touch, brushing the tears from
our faces. And the expansiveness of the promised life, for
which only pictures of wonderful, celebratory feasts will do.

Lord, it is Advent: I need to hear again your great
promises about the Last Things.
Lord, it is Advent: I need – penitently but hopefully – to
set my own life in the context of those Last Things –
both their judgement and their promise.

You promise me that there will be comfort for all the distresses, that they will fall away from us. And especially you promise us that our deepest grief – the death of loved ones; and our deepest fear – what our own dying may mean, will be gone for ever.

Death will not be part of the scheme of things ever again.

Lord, my spirit stretches to grasp that.
I can only glimpse its wonder, and be thankful.

You, Lord God of Judgement, promise us that all that disgraces us will be taken away from the earth.

Lord, my spirit stretches to grasp that, in Christ.
I glimpse and accept with wonder, and am thankful.

Lord God, you charged your people to wait for you: wait faithfully for you.
And to those who did, you sent your Son, and they knew him and were satisfied.
But still you ask us to wait, to see how surely the work of our Lord Jesus Christ will be fulfilled,

At the end of all things for all people.
(And in your destiny for me, your child.)

So in mind and spirit today I walk your holy mountain;
I give you praise
from a heart over-flowing.
For you have saved me all my life, and will save me to
the end,
And bring me to that joyous banquet
Which you will spread for all peoples,

All who with longing turn to you for help.
Amen.

For the Second Sunday of Advent, on or near Bible Sunday

'I live under the Word of God'[60]

I live under the Word of God
    – and I die under it too.
Your lively oracles, my Lord
        are still the compass of my way,
        the north, south, east and west
        I read for my life's safe voyaging.

My life's voyaging, safe
        though that requires dying?
Your Word, my God, is comfortable,
        for it speaks to my condition;
        not least because it asks of me surrender:
A giving-up of all that blurs
        the powerful imprint of your lettering
        upon what I do and am.

'When they lay me to rest, your Gospels
        will be open on my coffin';[61]
As, Lord, all my life
        they have lain upon the coffin
        of those seductions that distract
        from a life lived simply for you.

And yet they have comforted me, my Lord,
        comforted, fed, warmed and healed me,
        in the very moments of my dying
        to the things I thought I wanted,
        until your Word, your living Word

transformed my heart,
showing me a better way.

Lord God, as your living Word,
a two-edged sword, has pierced
between soul and spirit, making war
on all that would separate me from you,
So may that same living, loving Word
be with me when I face Death itself;
when, thrust by its devastation
from the warm companionships of this dear life
I stand alone, before the great Tribunal
and know myself judged.

O Lord God, your living Word, my Christ,
is then my trusted advocate, defending counsel,
my wholly trusted, living Lord, my Christ,
the one I met when first I read
the holy words of Scripture, knew his promise,
and took it for my own.

And so through him, even in death,
even in Death,
'I live, under the Word of God'
– and through the living Word of God,
– and in the living Word of God
for ever,

in Christ my Lord.
Amen.

For the Third Sunday in Advent

A vision from 'The Transfiguration'
by Edwin Muir

But he will come again, it's said, though not
Unwanted and unsummoned; for all things,
Beasts of the field, and woods, and rocks, and seas,
And all mankind from end to end of earth
Will call him with one voice. In our own time,
Some say, or at a time when time is ripe.
Then he will come, the Christ uncrucified,
Christ the discrucified, his death undone,
His agony unmade, his cross dismantled –
Glad to be so – and the tormented wood
Will cure its hurt and grow into a tree
In a green springing corner of young Eden,
And Judas damned take his long journey backward
From darkness into light and be a child
Beside his mother's knee, and the betrayal
Be quite undone and never more be done.[62]

O Sovereign God, the thought of your judgement on us fills us
with a holy fear. Like Adam we seek to hide, even to ourselves,
from the awfulness of our deserts. Even more, we seek to hide
from your just and pure gaze. And because we are so immersed
in our own condition we fail to understand what you sent your
Son to show us, that your divine judgements are always benign,
always to bring us through to good.

So this Advent day I thank you for this poet's wonderful vision
of the redeemed world transfigured at the end of time through
your powerful grace. Help me to grasp afresh that Judgement

Day is about your setting all things right, so that Adam unparadised finds himself again, wondering, in a young and green Eden: all that great load of loss and sin and wretched wrongness and wilful disobedience unwritten by the grace of Christ's mighty Cross. O Lord, help me to grasp that the same dynamic power which created the universes also confronted the worst that we are capable of and overcame it in space and time on that hill in Galilee; that same power which created, moved the gravestone and defeated death. That same power which created and saved can, and will, on Judgement Day, overturn the evils of history and restore us to be your loving and obedient children once more.

But you will not come, Lord, 'unwanted and unsummoned'. So, this Advent, I pray for that time to come when all of us and all Creation will call you with one voice, opening ourselves in trust to the Love which judges and sets things right. O Lord prepare my heart. O Lord, prepare your people. O Lord, prepare our world. Amen.

For the Fourth Sunday in Advent

The Last Enemy

And he who each day
reveals a new masterpiece of sky
and whose joy
can be seen in the eyelash of a child
who when he hears of our smug indifference
can whisper an ocean into lashing fury
and talk tigers into padding roars
This my God
whose breath is in the wings of eagles
whose power is etched in the crag of mountains
It is he whom I will meet
And in whose Presence I will find tulips and clouds
kneeling martyrs and trees
the whole vast praising of his endless creation
and he will grant the uniqueness
that eluded me
in my earthly bartering with Satan
that day when he will erase the painful gasps of my ego
and I will sink my face into the wonder of his glory love
and I will watch as planets converse with sparrows
On that day
when death is finally dead.[63]

This is my God, my God . . . It is you whom I shall meet and
in your presence find the whole vast praising of your endless
creation. It is you whom I shall meet and know, as now I only
glimpse, the glories of your love. And I shall take my part then
as I long to now, in the rejoicing of your creatures. I shall know
fully, as now I know only partially, what it is to be a part of

your wonderful and endless creating. Here I glimpse the full wonder of things, of which the promise of your Coming is but the rumour. O my Lord God, I offer my heart, to be prepared for the wonder of your coming to us this Christmas in simplicity as a child amidst your own creation; but more, I offer my heart to be prepared for the mysteries of your final Coming and for the wonders that lie ahead and are my destiny.

And there, with all I have loved of this world, I shall watch planets converse with sparrows in the glory of your presence. Prepare me, Lord! Amen.

For 1 December

December, with snowflakes and star,
In the inn of December, a fire,
A loaf, a bottle of wine,
Travellers, rich and poor, are on the roads.[64]

Lord, I have a journey to make this month: travelling to be done. I have to make preparations to meet you, even as you are travelling to meet me. Oh my Lord, the journey you made for me! From heaven your home, with its pure love and pure joy and unclouded presences, and its pure air of praise, to the clouded perceptions and faltering loves and ambiguous joys of our life. No journey I make can ever be a fraction as costly. Help me remember that as I begin my December travelling.

And as I start this journey, I thank you that indeed, whatever its hard snows, this month of December is hospitable, and an 'inn' its true image. For we are travelling towards your profound and gracious hospitality, Lord, and our welcoming of each other in our homes is but a little sign of that. Help me remember that on each festive occasion in the coming month.

I am but a poor traveller. But there will be poorer. Keep me mindful this month, Lord, of all those who are travelling it in harsh circumstances, and help me offer from what I have to assuage their need. And there will be other travellers I may meet who have been given wisdom beyond mine, to guide them. Help me hear them, and respond not with fear, like Herod, but with wonder and a heart receptive to new revelations of your love.

And at the last you are drawing me towards that only feast of food fit for me, a loaf and wine. Help me receive, oh my dear

Lord, all the love and safety, the grace and cherishing, that your Bread and your Wine offer me. So make this month of December a holy journey for me; and through me may other people find the road. Amen.

For Christmas tide (1)

One time of the year
the newborn child
is everywhere,
planted in madonna's arms . . .
naked or elaborately swathed . . .
lit by over-sized stars,
partnered with lambs,
bells, plastic camels in sets of three,
as if these were what we need
for eternity.

But Jesus the Man is not to be seen.
We are too wary, these days
of beards and sandalled feet.

Yet if we celebrate, let it be
that he
has invaded our lives with purpose,
overturning our cash-registers,
wielding his peace like a sword,
rescuing us into reality
demanding much more
than our shallow sentiment.
For become a Man, this babe will ask
all, of each of us.

And reaching out
always urgently with strong effective love
this Man will give his life and live again
For love of us.
O, let us adore him,
Christ – the Lord.[65]

I thank you, my Lord, for all the true delights of Christmas:

— the joy of planning gifts with care and love for those who will receive them
— the joy of festive gatherings where we seek each others' pleasure
— the joy of small children's wondering excitement
— the profound and beautiful joy as we worship in our candlelit churches.

I thank you for all these, Lord, and ask that you will keep my heart always open to them.

But my Lord, take me deeper into the holy mystery of your coming.
Let me understand how it was to draw me into eternity.
Let me see in this vulnerable, homeless infant the One he will become:

— In his manhood again vulnerable, for me.
— In his manhood again homeless, for me.
— In his manhood fighting evil with his peace, for me.
— In his manhood showing how inexhaustible the love of our Father God – for me.

You ask a gift of me, Lord: my trust.
My trusting of myself to your strong effective love.
O again this Christmas, my dear Lord, help me renew again
My creased and tattered trust,
and lay it by your manger, to go with you on your way,

Through Golgotha and beyond, to the glory of heaven rising.
Amen.

For Christmas tide (2)

Who has not considered Mary
　And who her praise would dim,
But what of humble Joseph
　Is there no song for him?

If Joseph had not driven
　Straight nails through honest wood
If Joseph had not cherished
　His Mary as he should;

If Joseph had not proved him
　A sire both kind and wise
Would he have drawn with favour
　The Child's all-probing eyes?

Would Christ have prayed, 'Our Father'
　Or cried that name in death
Unless he first had honoured
　Joseph of Nazareth?[66]

We don't ever fully know the consequences of the way we 'do' life and its relationships, do we, Lord?

I thank you for the 'Josephs' (not all of them male) in my life:

— the Joseph who taught me by example to do all work thoroughly and honestly
— the Joseph who taught me how trustworthy can be the loving commitment of marriage
— the Joseph who taught me how strong and gentle and protective can be parental love

— the Joseph who taught me the wisdom and integrity ordinary men and women are capable of in their untrumpeted lives
— the Joseph who taught me the name 'Father' to call on in life's bitter or hurtful experiences; yes, even in the final struggles of mortality.

Lord, thank you for my own special 'Josephs': I name them before you here: _____

Lord, thank you for all those who are being such as Joseph to someone at this moment. Lord, as parent or spouse, son or daughter, brother, sister, friend or fellow-worker: help me to be, in some way, a 'Joseph' for others. Today, and in the days to come. Amen.

For Christmas tide (3)

The Carol of Mary and the Apple

This ballad sprang from a detail in a short story by Ulrich Simon. Suppose the Serpent could have been made to weep? And thus the awful power of evil broken even in the Garden? It is another way of telling the story of our salvation . . .

Mary walked in winter
   Nine months long
Silent round her Eden
   No birds' song.

   Oh happy apple
   In Paradise bright
   When Eden was holy
   On Christmas night.

Eat! hissed the Serpent
   Taste delight
Warmth in the winter
   Music at night.

Eat! replied Mary
   Know in your blood
Sourness of evil
   Sweetness of good.

The Serpent bites:
   The apple bleeds
Across the snow
   Apple seeds.

At Eden's heart
   A sapling grows
Green around it
   Melting snows.

Bloom on the branches
   Red and white
Birds in the blossom
   Sing at night.

The bright-skinned Serpent
   Bowed his head
I knew not before
   How to weep, he said,

For silent birds
   Innocence fled
Blossom that falls
   Abel dead.

   Oh happy apple
   The Serpent bright
   Found Eden holy
   On Christmas night.

The Serpent writhes
   And casts old skin
The ice cracks wide
   Where seeds fall in.

Oh happy apple
In Paradise bright
When Eden was holy
On Christmas night.

Then weep! said Mary
   For joy in grief;
That sapling seeded,
   When grown to leaf,

Its richest fruit
   For this has kept:
To heal the hurt
   And meet the debt.

Creation stilled.
The Serpent wept.

Oh Earth that fruit
   For you grows fair:
With unbruised head
   The Serpent there

With beasts rejoices
   In Paradise bright;
In Eden, holy
   Since Christmas night.

Oh happy apple,
Tho' wintry our night,
Eden is holy
And Paradise bright.

Lord God, for the mystery of salvation which we begin to glimpse at Christmas, we thank you. For the promise of Creation restored, we thank you. For the overcoming of evil with good, and of death with life, we thank you. For the obedience of Mary and of all who have humbly lived and worked as you

have called them, that Eden may become holy, we thank you.
For our Lord Jesus Christ in whom is our hope, we thank you.

> For the means of grace and the hope of glory,
> we thank you.
> Amen.

For Christmas Eve • MORNING

The House of Christmas

To an open house in the evening
Home shall men come,
To an older place than Eden
And a taller town than Rome.
To the end of the way of the wandering star,
To the things that cannot be and that are:
To the place where God was homeless,
And all men are at home.[67]

'Home' . . . Lord, how deep our need of it, and how greatly, when
our homes are secure, we take them for granted. So, Lord, my
Lord who was himself homeless both as an infant and in his
ministry, I bring to you:

My thanks for the homes you have given me throughout
my life (through no virtue of my own)
— the home into which I was born, and the love that
awaited me
— the home of my childhood and youth, and its care and
protection
— the home I was first responsible for, and your blessing
of it
— the homes I have shared with others; their joys (and
sorrows)
— the home in which this day I come to another
Christmas.

Lord, in gratitude and love I thank you.

And I bring to you
> all those who this Christmas are
> without a home:
> — those who have lost their homes
>   through natural disasters
> — those who were driven from their
>   homes by war and terror
> — those who lost their homes through
>   poverty
> — those who were driven from their
>   homes by unkindness
> — those abandoning their homes
>   through folly
> — those who seek continually for a
>   home and cannot find one.

Lord, send them your help through their fellow human beings' concern and practical aid – and may I play my own part in such care.

And, Lord, I thank you that all the kindliness and security of the happiest home I have known is but a foreshadowing of that home I shall one day know with you; beyond all grief, beyond all transcendence, beyond anything that might harm or threaten, held in the loveliness of your presence. This Christmas Eve is your affirmation that this is your gift to us, O homeless one . . . So bring me home, Lord. Amen.

For Christmas Eve • NIGHT

Christmas Present

Midnight. The stillness of waiting.
After the hubbub, the noisy streets,
The frantic rush of hours
And sense of ill-preparedness,
We're caught as usual by the tyranny of time;
And the best we can manage will always be
A stable rather than smart hotel
To make our Christmas for our loved ones.
So we can do no more now, but wait:
While across the globe the moonlit silence spreads
Under the Christmas stars.
Wait, as the stillness spreads, spreads,
Across the world and into our hearts,
Into this stable, my heart.
A pinpoint in the vast dark
Of the waiting universe . . .
A lantern flickers in the shadows –
– The creatures there breathe softly, great eyes wide,
   They understand better than we that
   Unimaginable moments are upon us now –
Suddenly our planet will glow with a new brilliance
Among the revolving stars.
For the Light will come tonight
He will come again tonight
Into this poor stable, my heart.
So He – not I – will make Christmas for my loved ones.
For all the loved ones across the world
Their gift has come.

Dear Lord, be the one supreme gift tonight to your waiting world. May all our small tokens to each other speak of the overwhelming love of your Christmas gift to us. Amen.

For Christmas Day • MORNING (1)

O the magnitude of meekness!
　　Worth from worth immortal sprung;
O the strength of infant weakness
　　If eternal is so young! . . .

Nature's decorations glisten
　　Far above their usual trim;
Birds on box and laurel listen,
　　As so near the cherubs hymn . . .

God all-bounteous, all creative,
　　Whom no ills from good dissuade,
Is incarnate, and a native
　　Of the very world he made.[68]

A suddenly sharpened sense of the *reality*, indeed the *awefulness* – in the true sense of the word – of what Jesus did at Christmas. The utter otherness, largeness, holiness, joy and depth of heaven; and the physical miseries of human babyhood, the discomforts, cold, stench of blood and animal droppings, the rudeness and roughness of it all. We think the Cross was the costliest bit but surely *this*, this utter reduction and helplessness, was in its shocking diminishments, no less appalling and therefore no less a matter for wondering praise by the heavenly beings who saw and understood the 'magnitude of the meekness'. This self-confining of the unconfinable, within the bondage and limitations of our vulnerable, physically horizoned human life . . .

Yet because you came to loving arms, dear Jesus, heaven was connected. Because there were those who came with wonder and offered what they could, because Mary had given herself

for you, because Joseph had accepted the unbearable for a husband with grace, for you, the diagram of heaven's spacious and
lovely habitations were engraved on the earthen floor of that
rough shelter. And the song of the angels was not ironic: and
humanity's lesser music was echoing it truly, through those rafters
and beyond, to the throne of God the Father.

Lord, add my small carol to that song, as I kneel and wonder at the mystery of your gift to us. And keep me mindful always,
with deep thankfulness, of the perpetuity of Christmas in our
lives. Amen. Amen.

For Christmas Day • MORNING (2)

Prayers with those gathered to worship[69]

In the power of the Spirit, and in union with Christ, let us pray to the Father:

Father, on this holy day your Son our Saviour was born in human form; renew your Church as the body of Christ today;

And on this holy day, Christians the world over are celebrating his birth;

so open our hearts that he may be born in us, gathered here, today.

Lord, in your mercy
Hear our prayer.

Father, on this holy day there was no room for your Son in the inn, and Mary in the pain of labour brought him to birth; protect with your love those who today are without a home, or have seen their homes made derelict, or who live in deep poverty, pain, anxiety, sickness or distress.

Lord, in your mercy
Hear our prayer.

On this holy day shepherds in the fields heard good tidings of great joy; give us grace to share with others that same joy in your amazing love in our own day. And we pray for those for whom, amidst others' joy, this is a hard or bitter time of remembering or suffering; and those for whom your gift seems to offer little comfort; and those for whom this day has no holiness or glimpse of the wonder of your love. Thank you that your love is for all, and that you patiently await our acceptance.

Lord, in your mercy
Hear our prayer.

On this holy day the angels sang 'Peace to God's people on earth'; strengthen all those who work against the tides of hate, for peace and justice in the world; And on this holy day your Christ came as a light shining in the darkness; revisit with that light the darkness round Bethlehem today, and all such places of bitter strife.

Lord, in your mercy
Hear our prayer.

On this holy day, strangers found the Holy Family and saw the baby lying in the manger; bless *our* homes, our neighbours and all whom we love; and all strangers among us today.

Lord, in your mercy
Hear our prayer.

On this holy day, heaven is come down to earth and earth is raised to heaven; we remember all those who have died trusting in you: keep them in safety and with them, in the hope of heaven, all those who today will pass through death. Grant us with them to share in the joy of your eternal kingdom.

So, as on this holy day angels and shepherds worshipped at the manger-throne; receive the worship we offer today, with them and with all your saints through the ages.

Merciful Father,
accept these prayers
for the sake of your Son, our Saviour
Jesus Christ.
Amen.

For Christmas Night

At Bethlehem we must each imagine the scene for ourselves.
Was it a cave or a stable?
There is no way of knowing for certain.
The ox and the ass were the inspired interpretation of poets and
    others.
George Herbert added a horse and Christina Rossetti a camel.

One day the cave will become like a second ark;
No longer will the lion roar in the depths of the jungle.
Quiet as a shadow he will slide in and lie down with the
lambs and the mice in the rustling straw.[70]

So now, Lord, this evening, let me enter the holy shelter, where,
Mary and Joseph protecting you, you lie drowsily, your brilliant,
wondering, profound baby gaze drifting into your first infant
slumber. There is such peace here, Lord. After the haste and
distress of finding somewhere sheltering, the din and crush of
the crowds in the narrow streets, the clacketting of the woman
from the inn rushing to help when so suddenly Mary's time
was come, the knock of the beasts' hooves on the rough floor,
and the snorting of the family donkey restless for its food after
that journey – now, at last, among the slow heavy breathing of
the beasts, there is profound peace. Mary sleeps, her hand resting on the child lying quietly in the hay of the manger. Joseph
sleeps, his back against the door, legs stretched out; yet even in
slumber his spirit stretched alert for the cry of need. The beasts
sleep, resting from the hard-driven day.

    Soon the shepherds will arrive, just as dawn glimmers,
breathless with perplexed excitement and expectation. Soon there
will be all the world and its claims and its threats to face, that
world this infant has come to make his own and take home to

God. The long, hard, bitter journey stretches ahead. But for now, there is sleep.

And we too, after the excitements and delights and exhaustions of this Christmas Day, we too turn to sleep. And in our sleep, Lord, we join your infant slumbers in a dream; a dream of a place of havening, a shelter, that will one day be, where we shall all come who wish, and share the beasts' rest; where the creatures will share each others' peace, lion with lamb and mice, without any fear of destruction; where all that is predatory in our fellow-creatures – or in ourselves – will be gone for ever; where they shall not hurt or destroy in all your holy mountain, Lord. And to this peace, O my Lord, my little Lord Jesus – I thank you – through all that is to come, you, a little child, shall lead us. Lord, the glory of this dream that is a fact to come. That is your promise . . . underwritten by this sleeping infant here in this place. Sleep, little glorious Lord. I worship you. Amen.

For 28 December, the Holy Innocents, and times of dreadful disaster

This day sets before us, with peculiar intensity and sharpness, the strange character of this present world, with its mixture of joy and sorrow, promise and pain. Before the mystery of suffering we are silent. Our response is of a God who is not simply a spectator of the travail of creation, but One who in the cross of Christ has actually participated in that suffering.[71]

They are all dead, the little ones. O my Lord, they are all dead, the babies and the toddlers: through the centuries the small vulnerable ones lie in that last posture of brutalized sleep; and not just our children, Lord, but the small creatures. The dead blackbird that had crept for shelter beneath the waste-bin to die, the frozen sparrow, the thin starved city cat stretched in the gutter. Our cruelty, or simply our carelessness, combines with the destruct-ive forces of our natural world, and the little ones die.

And you don't stop it. You don't stop it.

Where were you, God, on that day in Bethlehem when those infants were torn from their mothers' anguished arms of protection and dashed down to death? Where were you when that bright blackbird died of poison behind our dustbin? Where were you when the great tsunami wave destroyed tens of thousands of lives and millions of livelihoods in Asia?

O my Lord Jesus Christ, this litany of loss. You haven't just sung it with us, you have lived it with us. Every hard stone that hurt your feet, every fallen sparrow your heart saddened over, every harsh repudiation you suffered, every verbal onslaught and brutal physical punishment you sustained, were *your* litany for *our* sorrow. So, Lord, what do *I* do with this heart-squeezing load of sorrow, of shame for our carelessness as a race and grief at natural calamity?

I follow your example, Lord, and share it all. I do not resist the grief in my heart as I see small bodies with their life and joy extinguished. I do not resist the shame in my heart as I see what my humanity does to suffering creatures. I do not resist the troubled perplexity welling up when I see bodies and lives broken by natural disasters. I take up the terrible reality and truth of such things – but, Lord, I do it with my hand in yours and my whole will and understanding looking for support in you. I look at *your* broken body, I hear the broken tones of *your* suffering, and I know I am held by a Lord who does not repudiate our suffering but knows it and shares it; by a Lord who not only shares it but goes through it to the sort of victory that seems unimaginable here in this place.

> *O Lord, for the joy that is set before us, give us faithfulness in the dark places.*
> *O Lord, for the joy that is set before **me**, give me faithfulness in the dark places.*

Help me today, Lord, to stand before the mystery of suffering alongside you, take its burden truthfully on to my flinching heart alongside you, and, held by your strength, affirm that here, even here, Jesus Christ is Lord.

To the glory of God the Father. Amen.

For 29 December

When the song of the angels is stilled
   When the star in the sky is gone
When the kings and princes are home
When the shepherds are back with their flocks
   the work of Christmas begins:
      to find the lost
      to heal the hungry
      to release the prisoners
      to rebuild the nations
      to bring peace among the people
      to make music in the heart.[72]

It's the one great religious festival here in this land that is as marked in its climax in its secular dimension as for those who celebrate the mystery at its core. For weeks the commercial world has banged its drum ever faster: for weeks the rhythm of preparation in street and home has grown more frenetic. Then it reached its climax, for faithful and unbelievers alike – and now we live in its aftermath.

Tidying the crumpled wrapping paper, finding space for the unwrapped and exclaimed-over presents, waving goodbye to the departing Christmas guests, savouring the simplicity of plain fare at meal-times, we pause at last to draw breath and contemplate the pilgrimage achieved.

Where have I travelled to, my Lord, over this festive season? What is reshaped within me – even if only a very little – by standing in the place I stood and seeing what I saw?

I stood in a place of achieved Love. Lord, I saw it, and I thank you.

For what more potent signal of completely selfless unconditional love could you give, than that of divine power abandoning its royalty of command, to lie a helpless infant, wholly dependent on the will and care of others, and subject to their thoughtlessness and cruelty?

And that is what I am left staring at, when all the trappings are gone. This fact in our human history, which has changed everything:

> And is it true? and is it true?
> This most tremendous tale of all,
> Seen in a stained-glass window's hue
> A Baby in an ox's stall?
> The Maker of the stars and sea
> Become a Child on earth for me?
> And is it true? For if it is . . .[73]

For if it is . . . then this is Love achieved beyond our dreaming. Divine and human love commingled and become one. Indeed, indeed, if this is true then the Christmas work has just begun and I must bestir myself about it.

On Boxing Day many parts of my Church celebrate remembrance of St Stephen, the first Christian martyr. Yesterday we remembered the death of the Holy Innocents. Today we remember Thomas à Becket, martyred at his altar in Canterbury. Love achieved is costly, costly, costly.

And so the Christmas work begun demands of me too, my infant Lord; not less than everything. Teach me, far beyond cards and gifts and Christmas hospitality, how to give when it costs; that with all who have glimpsed the astonishing mystery at the heart of Christmas I may take my part, today and into the future, in the Christmas work which has again this year, just begun, through the gift of God himself. Amen.

For New Year's Eve

A prayer for the year's ending, from John Henry Newman

Let us humbly and reverently attempt to trace God's guiding hand in the years we have hitherto lived. Let us thankfully commemorate the many mercies he has vouchsafed to us in time past, the many sins He has not remembered, the many dangers he has averted, the many prayers He has answered, the many mistakes he has corrected, the many warnings, the many lessons, the much light, the abounding comfort which He has from time to time given. Let us dwell upon times and seasons, times of trouble, times of joy, times of trial, times of refreshment . . . He has been all things to us. He has been . . . our God, our shield, and great reward, promising and performing, day by day. 'Hitherto hath He helped us.' 'He hath been mindful of us and will bless us'. He has not made us for naught; He has brought us thus far, in order to bring us further, in order to bring us to the end.[74]

I remember His care this year in times of trouble. Here I name some: _____

I remember His care this year in times of joy. Here I name some: _____

I remember His care this year in times of trial. Here I name some: _____

I remember His care this year in times of refreshment. Here I name some: _____

Lord God, thank you for all that was good in this year that is passing. Forgive what was wrong in it, both my own wrongdoing and other people's. Sanctify what was painful in it. And teach me to look back with thanksgiving, not nostalgia; and forward with faith and contentment. Through Jesus Christ your Son, our Lord. Amen.

For New Year's Day

Do all the good you can
By all the means you can
In all the ways you can
At all the times you can
To all the people you can
As long as you can.
(*Based on the Rule of John Wesley*)

He was pretty searching, wasn't he, Lord? Your servant John Wesley? Not just a brilliant preacher and a great man of prayer, but one who translated 'the way that leads to eternity' into what it means for us in the way we live. He offered, instead of the incipient revolution of violence, the silent revolution of understanding and living which comes from hearts wholly fixed on you.

Vision is needed, to remind us of what transforms the heart: renew as I need it my vision of you, Lord.

Faithfulness is needed, to stay thankfully within God's grace: renew as I need it my faithfulness to you, Lord.

Obedience is needed, to live in a way which speaks of you, and serves others: renew as I need it my obedience to your will for my life, Lord.

Love is needed, for all these: our fragile love for you, Lord, and your strong love of us; renew as I need it the depth and passion of my love for you, Lord, and O! do it by the urgent flow of your mighty love for me.

170

Then I shall, in your name, do all the good I can, as long as –
through you – I can. In the name of Christ in whom – only –
I can. Amen.

For Epiphany (1)

A prayer for late-comers, from *Helena,* by Evelyn Waugh

'Like me,' she said to them, 'you were late in coming. The shepherds were here long before; even the cattle. They had joined the chorus of angels before you were on your way . . .

'How laboriously you came, taking sights and calculating, where the shepherds had run barefoot! How odd you looked on the road, attended by what outlandish liveries, laden with such preposterous gifts! . . .

'Yet you came, and were not turned away. You too found room before the manger. Your gifts were not needed, but they were accepted and put carefully by, for they were brought with love. In that new order of charity that had just come to life, there is room for you, too. You were not lower in the eyes of the holy family than the ox or the ass.

'[And so] . . . you are the especial patrons of all latecomers, of all who have a tedious journey to make to the truth, of all who are confused with knowledge and speculation . . . of all who stand in danger by reason of their talents . . .

Dear cousins, pray for me . . .'[75]

Dear Lord, thank you for this new order of charity which makes room for us all. Thank you for finding room for me before the manger, delayed though my coming was. And this Feast of Epiphany I pray for all who labour to come to you but find the way hard and the road long and doubts and hesitations like so much outlandish livery hampering their movement. Draw them to the Epiphany light brightening the door of that small place we must stoop to enter, as – how inconceivably! – you yourself stooped. So that in the one place where incompatibilities are united, the learned and the donkeys, the rough workers and the sophisticated court servants, the sheep and goats, oxen and astrologers and sky-gazing country-folk may all find their worship – and each others' – accepted. And know themselves equally blessed.

And may I lay down, at your Epiphany cradle, all that in me would make any feel unwanted or unworthy or inappropriate in such a place. That as the holy family accepted the ox and the ass and the shepherds and the magi and me, so may I add my own wondering welcome to all who wistfully peer in at this door. In thankfulness for the Love that guided my own stumbling footsteps. Amen.

For Epiphany (2)

At the close of Epiphany tide

Our God, heaven cannot hold him
   nor earth sustain;
heaven and earth shall flee away
   when he comes to reign:
in the bleak mid-winter
   a stable place sufficed
the Lord God Almighty
   Jesus Christ . . .
What can I give him,
   poor as I am?
If I were a shepherd
   I would bring a lamb;
if I were a wise man
   I would do my part;
yet what I can I give him –
   give my heart.[76]

It's all here, isn't it, my breath-taking mind-blowing stupendous Lord of Love? The whole vast beyondness of Advent, demanding that we uncover our heads and make ourselves face what is beyond us to grasp, only just possible for us to glimpse, the vastness of that Majesty and Authority which is yours, Lord, by nature and right. Yet so intimately concerned with us, small and insignificant as we are, puffing ourselves up like children in adult clothes too big, as we strut about the universe.

'Heaven and earth shall flee away' when you come to reign. That is the true scale of things, my Lord God, and that is what Advent reminds me.

174

And yet, this Christmas when you came to reign, you crossed eternity with time and chose to enter our human scale of things. You entered at the lowest end of that scale, so that what we thought adequate care for our creatures, cattle and donkey, you chose for yourself and slept there in the straw among them, one with the lowliest.

O my dear generous greatly-gentle Lord, I kneel by you in that straw myself. With my hand on the sleeping donkey's rough flank, and my breath merging with the sweet heavy breathing of the cattle, I kneel beside you in wonder and tears. Wonder at the magnanimity of your meekness, wonder at the sort of Lord you are and always have been and always will be. Tears that you came thus because only so could you show us – show me – the truth of the God we worship and have so often misrepresented. O my dear Lord, reach deeply into my heart and shape it to this lowly scene.

Lord, I know that what matters to you is not your own sacrifice but how we respond. At Christmas we respond to tenderness by offering such gifts as we have, wise men and shepherds and the rest of us somewhere in between. They came and gave to you, and so, O my Lord, with great yearning, so must I. So I bring all those parts of my life I have insensibly taken back under my own control; and those desires and indulgences which have deflected me from your way; and most of all that defended unshared centre into which no one, not even my dearest, is admitted. Great Master of the Universe, my heart is so narrow and small at its centre that it cannot accommodate greatness. But there is room enough in it for a child: a small, sleeping, helpless baby. O my Lord, take shelter in this heart and make it your own. Amen. Amen.

For January

Religion is in the heart
Not in the knees.[77]

The Living Christ still has two hands,
one to point the way,
and the other held out to help us along.[78]

Lord, I do find this bit of the year so hard. It's cold and grey, and Christmas and New Year and Epiphany are past. We took the decorations down and the rooms looked tidy but bare; and we put away all the presents, and suddenly it all seemed a sort of fantasy, a dream world that we'd escaped to, which was not for the everyday.

So, dear Lord who came not to a decorated room and crowds singing your praise, but to a workaday, prosaic ordinary way of life, help me to make my Christ-mass now, today, in the sort of life you actually came to. Help me to pick up the load of ordinary toil I must struggle with, and feel so reluctant to face. Help me to follow up all the good intentions of care for others – especially any I've newly heard from this Christmas-tide. Help me to settle to the routine of life again, Lord, and not hanker after the indulgences of the holiday season. Help me to be aware of *others'* struggles, and pray for them and hold out my hands to help.

And all over the world there are those for whom the respite has been all too brief, if it's occurred at all. I hold before you, Lord God, our Father, all those who today are destitute of shelter, food, work, or hope: I hold before you, Lord Jesus, all those who have never met you, or do not know your name or of what you have given us through your coming: I hold before you, Lord and Holy Spirit, all those who seek to work for good but lack the strength or will to achieve it; all those who struggle with their own temptations and do not know whence help may come to strengthen them. And where happiness and reasons for living seem utterly destroyed, by bereavement or loss in its many kinds, living Christ, use my two hands to work for you, and use my heart as a channel of your love.

For Christ-mass sake. Amen.

Epilogue
For the darkness of the unknown way ahead

'I am the Light of the world'

It was just a nightlight, Lord. A nightlight on a saucer
Its tiny flame warming the darkness, pushing the shadows
  back . . .
But I thought of you, and what you meant when you said
'I am the Light of the world' . . .
In our souls, Lord,
You are the thankful dawn after long black night;
You are the radiance of sunlight when all was lightless grey.
In our souls, Lord,
You are the play of light on the windy leaves,
The glancing brilliance on the waters,
The sunlight tipping the distant mountains
Telling us day is come.
Then I remembered, Lord, that I don't have to wait for the
  dawn.
For when life is thick black, and dawn nowhere near,
You are that little bud of flame, my nightlight, pushing the
  shadows back.

I thought of the small lamps you knew as a child,
In Galilee, in nights in Galilee
Watching your mother light the house with that small brave
  flame.
(And early you knew you would yourself bring Light to us
  all:

The people who walked in darkness shall see a great light . . .)

And I thought of the candles we light in the dark of our
  hearts' grief.
Candles for prayers in holy places,
Candles in hasty home-built shrines amid the wilting flowers:
Claiming the light even when grief is most dark,
In some profound and simple way enacting that ultimate
  triumph of Light
In the face of death itself.

And last, Lord, I thought of all those celebratory candles.
The candles we light festively . . .
The great surge of Advent light
Rolling back the darkness through our churches and
  cathedrals,
Proclaiming the end to come of long-endured darkness
In the glory of eternal Light.
And then the candles lit in our homes at festive meals, and
  on our Christmas trees,
And finally, finally, Lord,
The glory of the Light shining from a crib, and from the
  stable door
Lighting up our homes, wherever we go, and where we
  worship you.
Carolling lanterns in the frosty night, and elegant candles
  held by choirboys,
Simple tapers in the hands of humble worshippers,
Eagerly, longingly, crowding to that door
Where the source of Light lies.

It was only a nightlight, Lord:
But it reminded me I have only to claim it in this bit of my
  life,

For a small brave flame to glow there in the dark.
So today, Lord, wherever and whenever darkness threatens,
I light your candle and claim your Light.

Now, Lord. Right here, Lord. Amen.

Envoi

Ghostly gladness

May you lead your life in light-heartedness,
Keep loneliness far away;
May gloom not remain with you,
But may God's cheerfulness
Forever sing out merrily in your life.[79]

Notes

All material not otherwise designated is by Ruth Etchells.

1. Albert Radcliffe, 'Texture', in *Third Way*, Vol. 28, No. 4, May 2005.
2. R. S. Thomas, 'The Belfry', in Christopher Cocksworth and Rosalind Brown, *Being a Priest Today: Exploring Priestly Identity*, Canterbury Press, 2002.
3. St Augustine, quoted in *The Hodder Book of Prayers in Large Print*, ed. Rosemary Curtis, Hodder and Stoughton, 1997.
4. H. Van der Looy, the Brakkenstein Community of Blessed Sacrament Fathers, 'Following Jesus', in *Rule for a New Brother*, trans. the Benedictine Nuns of Cockfosters, Darton, Longman and Todd, 1973, 1977.
5. From Christopher Cocksworth and Rosalind Brown, 'Being for Prayer', in *Being a Priest Today*, see note 2.
6. Richard Gillard, 'Brother, sister, let me serve you' (The Servant Song), © copyright 1977 Scripture in Song (a Div of Integrity Music Inc.), Sovereign Music UK, P.O. Box 356, Leighton Buzzard LU7 3WP, UK. Reproduced by permission. See *New Hymns and Worship Songs*, Kevin Mayhew, 2001.
7. Lancelot Andrewes, in *A Treasury of Prayer*, compiled by Tony Castle, Hodder and Stoughton, 1983.
8. 'The Last Word', mistakenly attributed to Sandra Duguid (true author unknown), in *The Lion Christian Poetry Collection*, compiled by Mary Batchelor, Lion, 1995.
9. Janet Lees, in *The Hodder Book of Prayers in Large Print*, see note 3.
10. From the writings of Austin Baker, Benedictine monk 1574–1641, in *The Lion Book of Prayers*, compiled by Mary Batchelor, Lion, 1993.
11. Prayer in Church Missionary Society (CMS) *Prayerletter*, April, 1999, adapted from Henry Venn's leading principles for CMS.
12. R. S. Thomas, 'The Bright Field', quoted in *The Nation's Favourite Poems of Journeys*, BBC Books, 2000.
13. Prayer for Hawaii, CMS *Prayerletter*, October, 1999.

14. Carmen Bernos de Gasztold, *Prayers from the Ark*, trans. Rumer Godden, Macmillan, 1963.

15. Adapted from a prayer by Beryl Bye, in *A Treasury of Prayer*, see note 7.

16. Dag Hammarskjöld, from *Markings*, trans. W. H. Auden and Leif Sjöberg, Faber and Faber, 1964; quoted in *A Treasury of Prayer*, see note 7.

17. From CMS *Prayerletter*, June, 1999.

18. 'Moving House' by Jan Sutch Prickard from *Maker's Blessing, Prayers and Meditations from the Iona Community*, published by Wild Goose Publications, 2000, http://www.ionabooks.com.

19. Gumley House School pupil, in *A Treasury of Prayer*, see note 7.

20. Found on the walls of a cave in Cologne where Jews had been hiding; on page 184 of *Holocaust Poetry*, trans. and ed. Hilda Schiff, Fount/HarperCollins, 1995.

21. Thomas Traherne, 'Wonder', in his *Centuries, Poems, and Thanksgivings*, ed. H. M. Margoliouth, Clarendon Press, 1958.

22. Amy Carmichael, *Gold Cord*, SPCK, 1932.

23. Prayer from Nigeria, CMS *Prayerletter*, May, 2001.

24. Prayer of the Venerable Bede, quoted in CMS *Prayerletter*, Christmas Eve, 1999.

25. David Scott, 'Valley Road, Louisville', in David Scott, *Piecing Together*, Bloodaxe Books, 2005. Reproduced by permission of the publisher.

26. Austin Farrer, 'The One Genius: Words for Life', in *The Hodder Book of Prayers in Large Print*, see note 3.

27. One of the earliest Christian prayers recorded, in *The Lion Book of Famous Prayers*, Lion, 1983.

28. John Keble, 'New every morning is the love', in *Hymns Ancient and Modern New Standard*, Canterbury Press, 1983, 1988.

29. Andrew Marvell, from 'Bermudas – Song of the Emigrants', in *The Faber Book of Religious Verse*, ed. Helen Gardner, Faber and Faber, 1972.

30. Felicity Prescott, in *Christian*.

31. R. S. Thomas, 'Pilgrimages', *Collected Poems, 1945–1990*, Dent, 1993.

32. Anonymous prayer from the sixteenth century, set to music by Thomas Tallis; from pew leaflet, Durham Cathedral.

33. Archbishop Helder Camara, 'King's Son', *Into Your Hands, Lord*, Darton, Longman and Todd, 1987.

34. Joachim Jeremias, quoted in *Health and Healing*, No. 17, Epiphany, 1988.

35. Oriah Mountain Dreamer, 'The Dance', quoted by Mark Tully in *Something Understood*, BBC Radio 4, 1 January 2006.

36. Judy Hirst, *Struggling to be Holy*, Darton, Longman and Todd, 2006.

37. Old English rhyme, in *A Treasury of Prayer*, see note 7.

38. David Scott, 'Cædmon's Song', in David Scott, *Piecing Together*, see note 25.

39. From John Pritchard, *Living Easter Through the Year*, SPCK, 2005.

40. David Scott, 'Don't', in David Scott, *Piecing Together*, see note 25.

41. 'How Terrible' by Ruth Burgess from *Maker's Blessing*, see note 18.

42. R. S. Thomas, 'Gift', *Experimenting with an Amen*, Macmillan, 1993.

43. Cliff Ashby, 'Stranger in this Land', *Plainsong: Collected Poems*, Carcanet Press Ltd, 1985. Reproduced by permission of the publisher.

44. Israel Abrahams, based on Solomon Gabriel (eleventh century), in *Prayers and Meditations*, ed. Peter Washington, Everyman edn, David Campbell, 1995.

45. George MacDonald, in *The Lion Book of Famous Prayers*, see note 27.

46. Thomas John Carlisle, 'The Great Intruder', in *The Lion Christian Poetry Collection*, see note 8.

47. The Venerable Bede, 'For Protection', in *The Fount Book of Prayer*, ed. Robert van der Weyer, HarperCollins, 1973.

48. Carmen Bernos de Gasztold, 'The Prayer of the Goat', *Prayers from the Ark*, see note 14.

49. David Scott, 'The Meadow, a Soul', in David Scott, *Piecing Together*, see note 25.

50. David Scott, 'The Meadow, a Soul', in David Scott, *Piecing Together*, see note 25.

51. Prayer from Bangladesh, in John Carden, *A Procession of Prayers*, SCM Press, 1998.

52. Sydney Carter, 'Mother Teresa', in *The Lion Christian Poetry Collection*, see note 8.

53. Archbishop Alcuin of York (755–804), in *More Latin Lyrics*, trans. Helen Waddell, Gollancz, 1976, 1985.

54. Evangeline Paterson, 'Miss Pettigrew and Tree', in *The Lion Christian Poetry Collection*, see note 8.

55. 'Will you come and follow me?' (verse 1 of 5). Words: John L. Bell and Graham Maule, © 1987, WGRG, Iona Community, Glasgow G2 3DH.

56. Richard Crashaw, 'The Widow's Mites', *Poems*, ed. L.C. Martin, Clarendon Press, 1957.

57. Kathy Galloway, 'Time to Go' (adapted from Psalm 139), *Talking to the Bones*, Triangle/SPCK, 1996.

58. Isaac of Stella, quoted by the Revd Liz Culling in 'The Spiritual Director', in the *Church of England Newspaper*, 8 March 2002.

59. From a letter written by the monk Fra Giovanni to the Contessa Allagia della Aldobrandeschi, in Florence, dated Christmas Eve, *Anno Domini* 1513.

60. Pope John Paul II's self-description.

61. At Pope John Paul II's funeral, the gospels were literally laid open on his coffin.

62. Edwin Muir, from 'The Transfiguration', *Collected Poems*, Faber and Faber, 1960.

63. Stewart Henderson, 'The Last Enemy', in *Assembled in Britain: Poems So Far 1972–1986*, Marshall Pickering, 1986. Reprinted by permission of HarperCollins Publishers Ltd © Stewart Henderson 1986.

64. George Mackay Brown, 'The Dance of the Months', in *The Lion Christian Poetry Collection*, see note 8.

65. Luci Shaw, 'One Time of the Year', *The Secret Trees*; quoted in *The Lion Christian Poetry Collection*, see note 8.

66. Gilbert Thomas, 'Who has not considered Mary', quoted by Rosemary Hartill in *Readings for Christmas*, BBC World Service, December 2002.

67. G. K. Chesterton, 'The House of Christmas', *Collected Poems*, Cecil Palmer, 1927.

68. Christopher Smart, from Hymn 32, *Hymns and Spiritual Songs for the Feasts and Festivals of the Church of England*; collected in *The New Oxford Book of Christian Verse*, ed. Donald Davie, Oxford University Press, 1981.

69. Intercessions written for Christmas Day Eucharist, Durham Cathedral.

70. Neville Braybrooke, 'The Wise Men', *Four Poems for Christmas*, Pauline Press, 1986.

71. John Polkinghorne, 'Holy Innocents' Day', *Living in Hope*, SPCK, 2003.

72. Howard Thurman, 'Christmas begins', in the Archbishop of Canterbury's Christmas card, 1995.

73. John Betjeman, 'Christmas', *Collected Poems*, John Murray, 1958, 1962.

74. John Henry Newman, sermon on 'Remembrance of Past Mercies', *Parochial and Plain Sermons, Vol. 5, 1840–1869* (Newman website). Grateful acknowledgement to Anne and Jamie Harrison and Joan Crooks for this material.

75. Evelyn Waugh, *Helena*, Penguin, 1950/1963. Reproduced by permission of the publisher.

76. Christina Rossetti, 'In the Bleak Mid-winter', in *Hymns Ancient and Modern New Standard*, see note 28.

77. Douglas Jarrold, in *Hodder Book of Prayers in Large Print*, see note 3.

78. T. W. Mason, in *Hodder Book of Prayers in Large Print*, see note 3.

79. Richard Rolle, 'Ghostly Gladness', in *Praying with the English Mystics*, compiled and introduced by Jenny Robertson, Triangle/SPCK, 1990.

Thematic Index

Author Index

Paterson, Evangeline 122–3
Polkinghorne, John 164
Prescott, Felicity 56
Prickard, Jan Sutch 28
Pritchard, John 84

Radcliffe, Albert ix–x
Rolle, Richard 181
Rossetti, Christina 174

Schiff, Hilda (trans.) 32
Scott, David 46, 82, 86, 112, 113

Shaw, Luci 147
Smart, Christopher 158

Thomas, Gilbert 149
Thomas, R. S. x, 14, 60, 92
Thurman, Howard 166
Traherne, Thomas 36

Venn, Henry *see* Church Missionary Society

Waugh, Evelyn 172
Wesley, John 170

The Society for Promoting Christian Knowledge (SPCK) was founded in 1698. Its mission statement is:

To promote Christian knowledge by

- **Communicating the Christian faith in its rich diversity;**

- **Helping people to understand the Christian faith and to develop their personal faith; and**

- **Equipping Christians for mission and ministry.**

SPCK Worldwide serves the Church through Christian literature and communication projects in over 100 countries, and provides books for those training for ministry in many parts of the developing world. This worldwide service depends upon the generosity of others and all gifts are spent wholly on ministry programmes, without deductions.

SPCK Bookshops support the life of the Christian community by making available a full range of Christian literature and other resources, providing support for those training for ministry, and assisting bookstalls and book agents throughout the UK.

SPCK Publishing produces Christian books and resources, covering a wide range of inspirational, pastoral, practical and academic subjects. Authors are drawn from many different Christian traditions, and publications aim to meet the needs of a wide variety of readers in the UK and throughout the world.

The Society does not necessarily endorse the individual views contained in its publications, but hopes they stimulate readers to think about and further develop their Christian faith.

For further information about the Society, visit our website at *www.spck.org.uk* or write to:
SPCK, 36 Causton Street,
London SW1P 4ST, United Kingdom.